ALL THE PATHS
OF THE LORD ARE
MERCY AND TRUTH

By Abram and Maria Hamm

Translation of the book:

DIE WEGE DES

HERRN SIND

LAUTER GUTE

By Abram and Maria Hamm

"The Paths of the Lord are Mercy and Truth"
Psalm 25:10

(Photo on the cover, The house of Abram Hamm's family in Karguj, the Orenburger district of the Southern Ural Mountains.

ALL THE PATHS OF THE LORD ARE MERCY AND TRUTH

By Abram and Maria Hamm

Living Sacrafice Books

P.O. Box 443
Bartlesville, OK 74005
U.S.A.

Abram and Maria Hamm in Germany in 1985.

Author's Foreword

"He that observeth the wind shall not sow; and he that regardeth the clouds shall not reap." Ecclesiastes 11:4

Since the time of the earthly pilgrimage is inclining to its end, we have been repeatedly admonished to write down what we have experienced in the U.S.S.R. with our Lord.

We did not want these precious experiences to be just taken with us to the grave, but rather that they be preserved, for other people, especially our children and grandchildren.

Although we hardly felt ourselves in a situation to record every detail of what we experienced, we have dared to try it with prayer for God's blessing and help. In many things we were thrown back on our memories, since we were unable to make many notes while we were still in the U.S.S.R.

The paths in which our Lord directed us, we were not always able to understand, yet we can now witness to God's glory that He allowed all to come to pass for our good. This was true even of the hunger and suffering in the years of starving, the forced labor, the imprisonment in the camps, and the persecution by the authorities.

The wise Solomon has said, only he who ventures something can win. As little members of the body of Christ in the U.S.S.R. we experienced the truth of this. We can rejoice now that we went this way and not an easier one.

Each one who has truly entrusted himself to the Lord, and left the broad road of destruction, in order to be a disciple on the narrow road that leads to the homeland above, will be permitted to prove His goodness and mercy.

Schosz Holte, May 1985
Abram and Maria Hamm

Translator's Introduction

It was an honor and a pleasure to be asked to translate this fine book by Abram and Maria Hamm. Brother Hamm was personally in our congregation and our home, on a visit to Ohio. We found his message and his life inspiring.

Later, on a visit to Germany, we had the privilege of being in Brother Hamm's church and home. We enjoyed the warm fellowship there, too.

I was impressed by the message of this book, which records for posterity the sufferings and triumphs of the evangelical Christians behind the Iron Curtain.

Abram Hamm was called as a young man to serve his Lord in sharing the Word, especially with children and youth. Because the communist government fiercely persecuted this kind of work, Brother Hamm was arrested in 1967, and sentenced to one and a half years in a concentration camp. His continued resistance to a watered-down gospel, and the leftist ideology brought him in 1970, a second term in the camps; this time for three years.

Abram's wife, Maria, has always stood loyally by his side. She did not hesitate when he was in the prison camps, even under threats and fines, to offer her house for congregational meetings.

One feels that this book was written with much prayer. May it serve the readers as a blessing, as it speaks of the testimony of the believing and suffering congregations in the U.S.S.R.

Table of Contents

Part III: Abram and Maria Hamm: Life Together

Part I

Maria Hamm (born Braun): Childhood and Youth

Chapter 1

Expropriation, Loss of Rights and Hunger

In the village of Kamenka Number Four, in the South Ural Mountains, my parents lived, — Gerhard Braun and Kathrina (born Regier). They were Godfearing and industrious farmers. They farmed 65 hectares of plowland and God's blessing rested on their work.

For my parents, the Bible verse in Proverbs 10:22 applied well: "The blessing of the Lord, it maketh rich, and he addeth no sorrow with it." Nine children were born to them — seven remained living. And they regarded the chilren as a gift of God.

I, Maria, was born on the 4th of May, 1927. We children could cheerfully romp about in our beautiful dwelling house. Beside it stood a stable, barn and blacksmith's shop. In addition, we owned a bath house, a special building standing apart on the courtyard.

In the adjoining garden, vegetables were raised and many berry bushes stood there. Six horses had enough to do with plowing, sowing and harvest. In the stables we also had eight milk cows, several beef cattle and a bunch of pigs. From our seventy sheep, we had enough wool for our own use as well as for sale. Many chickens, geese, and ducks provided us eggs, roast fowl and soup stock.

For so much work, my father constantly had a hired hand and a maid for the house. Our agricultural machinery included some plows, harrows, sowing machines, mowing machine, and a harvester. With the gathering in of the harvest we always hitched up several wagons.

In the years, 1929 and 30, the Communist Party decided to put together all the individual farms and convert them to collective farms. The land was taken from the farmers; also the livestock and the farm tools and machinery. Many farmers were imprisoned and sent to Siberia. Whole families were dragged away. Many of them died of hunger and cold, never seeing their homes again.

On the 6th of January, 1930, it became our family's turn. Suddenly our cattle and horses were taken. We were only allowed to keep one cow. Our hay and straw piles were taken away, then our tools and machinery. On March 27, 1930, my father was sent to jail without any proof of wrongdoing. Later, he died there in April, 1933. He never saw his family again.

Now Mother was alone with our seven children. The oldest was 15, and the youngest barely 2 years old. It was very hard to feed this large family. We had no money to buy food, and my mother dared not work away to earn anything.

It got worse. On January 9, 1932, we were ordered to leave our house within two hours. Even the last cow was taken away from us. Where should we go now? Outside a strong snowstorm raged, and icy coldness. In her helplessness, my mother wrung her hands and cried out to God for help, — he who is a father to widows and orphans. God heard her supplications and sent her brother Jakob.

Our uncle took us all up into his house. With tears Mother thanked both God and her brother. We still had a roof over our heads and did not have to wander like so many others, miserable and helpless in the north woods, freezing and starving.

We were permitted to take some small furniture with us-beds, dresser, table and stools. But all our supplies of wheat, rye and barely were confiscated.

Now began a very difficult time for us. Mother lost her civil rights and could get no work, and we children were not allowed to attend school. As children of the "privileged classes", we had no claim to any education and could not train for any profession. Finally, the hard winter went by. Then we children could at least go out into field and forest to look for food. My brothers trapped small animals, skinned them, and brought them to mother who cooked or brewed them into soup. When the birds had built their nests, my brothers climbed up into the trees and gathered the eggs, which gave us some nourishing food.

We girls gathered wild plants, like carrots and sorrel, and picked wild forest berries. That was at times rather dangerous because we occasionally choose inedible and poisonous plants and then had to violently vomit. From time to time sympathetic neighbors had pity on us and brought us a few small potatoes or a little bowl of skimmed milk.

Our mother suffered the most during this scarcity. She could not bear to look on when we children cried from hunger. She often denied herself of the last mouthfull in order to save it for us children. We two youngest girls, Anna and I often ran to the village to visit other children. There many times a little bit of food was given to us, for some people had sympathy for us thin children.

It was always the worst in the winter time, because then one could find nothing outside, whether plants or mice or birds' eggs. On one cold winter's day — I was just six years old — Mother had made a gruel out of millet leaves and bran and salt and then baked it into "cutlets". She served this with a soup made from dried herbs and chives. My little cousin Maria came by and wondered what kind of good smelling dish this was. She wanted to trade places with me and proposed, "Maria, you eat with us today, and I'll eat with you!"

I was at once agreed, for I knew the difference. At my aunt's I recieved a piece of buttered bread and a mug of milk that tasted wonderful. I was not yet finished eating when Marie came running back, weeping, "I can't eat that! I thought it was really cutletts or chops! But that stuff I can't even swallow!" Now I was afraid that I would not be allowed to eat anymore and began to stand up to leave the table. But then my uncle said, "Just eat your fill!" and he began to tease his daughter about the delicious "cutletts".

Although it went better for our uncle, he very seldom gave anything to our mother. However, our aunt, now and again secretly gave us something to eat.

From former times, mother had two gold finger rings and a gold watch. She wanted to sell these valuables but nobody took them because money was scarce. Then mother found out that there was a store in Torsin that bought up gold items. She sent the rings and the watch there and received for them seventy pounds of rye flour. Out of that she baked bread. Daily she cut 7 ounces of bread for each of the little children and 14 ounces for the bigger children. That was not much, but at least it was bread and not chaff. Mother had already traded away all our good clothes. Now our whole family wore only faded, patched clothes.

Mother would gladly have visited our father in prison, but the money was lacking. One day the postman brought her a letter. We were all anxious to know what news had come from father. He wrote of his great homesickness and asked for a family photo. Especially he longed for us two youngest ones, and often dreamed about us. And when he would wake from his dreaming he would cry for a long time. He reported also that he was very weak and sick. He had a stomach ulcer that gave him great pain. He could hardly keep any food down. His brother Johnann was in the same prison, so they could encourage one another and share joys and sorrows.

With great difficulty, we found somebody to photograph our family. Six times one letter after another, my mother sent Father letters with our family photo in them. But not one of them arrived. Finally we found someone who could bring Father our family picture. His joy over it was indescribably great.

One day in 1933, David Abrams came and asked for the hand of my oldest sister Katharina. She had now become 18 years old. David had worked earlier on our farm. Mother would have liked to keep Katharina with us, because she thought she was still too young to marry. She wrote to Father and asked his counsel. He answered that Katharina was still quite young, but he had to think also how hard a struggle our family was having. Therefore he could not really oppose the marriage. David came from a good family and was an industrious and orderly person.

The wedding took place a little later in a small family gathering. At first the young married pair lived in the house of David's parents. As a skilled tractor driver, David earned good wages and soon was able to build a small house of his own with his young wife.

Our family got back our civil rights in 1932, and was permitted to work at the collective farm. But that fell very heavily on my mother, because she was so weak and starved. We children were again allowed to attend school.

As the 27th of March, 1933 neared, our Mother reminded us how it was exactly three years ago that Father was arrested. As the next to the youngest, I could hardly remember my Father. I recalled only how he loved to play hide-and-seek with us. Otherwise I knew nothing about my Father. At the time he was arrested, I was barely three years old!

As Easter time neared again, my Mother would have liked to prepare us a treat, as she had always done earlier—but where would she get the money to do so? She told us Bible stories instead, and sang Easter songs with us.

Uncle Jakob hung up a swing in the cool summer kitchen, and there his children and we could play. We also sang old favorite songs and repeated them over and over. My 13 year old sister Lena built our little band of children into a real chorus. She stood in front of us and gave the tune from an old tuning fork.

We children lived unworriedly as long as we had something to eat and could be with our Mother. Outside the snow was thawing and this made deep water puddles. So we did not dare to go out because we got wet too easily, and had no clothes to change into. So we busied ourselves in our room with homemade games, cardboard and carrots.

On such a day, our postman came again. But this time Uncle Johann had bad news for us — our father had died on April 20, 1933. That was a bitter blow. Mother was almost ready to give up and we children wept unconsolably, because we would never more see our Father on earth. But then Mother could comfort us, "Dear children, we have still one hope — we shall see Father again in heaven. There is no more hunger up there, no sickness, no pain, and no parting!"

Up until now my Mother still always hoped and waited for the return home of our father, so that then everything would once again go better. But now all earthly hope had perished. She grieved day and night and finally became seriously ill. Some neighbor ladies visited her, also Aunt Lena, who was sort of the village person in charge of first aid..

My Mother developed, besides the general weakness, a painful ulcer in her throat and because of that had trouble even breathing. Aunt Lena tore a feather from a hen and used it to paint my mother's throat with birch teas.

We children moaned and wept and had to be moved to another room. Then my sister Lena said, "Our Papa has died now. What shall we do if Mama dies, too?"

In her weakness, my Mother pled with the Lord, "Give me strength so that I can get up again, and take care of the children. And yet another request I have, please let me live long enough until the youngest, Anna, is 18 years old." God had mercy on her misery, and let Mother get well again. We were all thankful. Some time later, the aunt with whom we lived sickened and died. She left her husband and seven children with no one to look after them. The youngest was one year old and the oldest 14.

Uncle Jakob married again, to a widow with 5 children and moved after the wedding with his seven children into the house of his second wife. He sold his own home and lent my mother a sum enough to buy a little cottage near her parents. It also had a garden, in which she could plant potatoes and vegetables, so that feeding the family could become easier. My bigger brothers and sisters worked in the collective farm and earned something, too.

My Mother was anxious that we children could celebrate Christmas, despite all the poverty. She taught us Christmas songs and had us learn little poems. She dressed up the dolls in different clothes, secretly, and at Christmas lay them like new beside our holiday plates. On the plates also lay a sweet that Mother had made from potato flour and syrup. There was even a Christmas tree — it was a broom, set up side down and decorated!

We children had cut out various figures from paper, which served as tree ornaments. Mother fetched carrots out of the cellar, which we carved into various figures. With these things we had much fun and the time went quickly, until we had to go and sleep.

In the winter of 1935, Uncle Johann was released from his imprisonment. On the next day he visited us. We all sat around him and he took Anna and me on his knees. Then he told of the hard time in the prison, how it had gone with Father, and about his sickness and death.

He even knew the last words of the dying man. Father was an impressive man with a weight of 220 pounds. But at the end he weighed only 70 pounds! He was buried in the prison cemetery.

In 1937 Uncle Johann was arrested again. Since then, nobody found any trace of him. My Mother at least was thankful to know exactly how my father had died.

Chapter 2

Little Joys of Childhood

I n the year 1934, I was supposed to go to school. But I had such
worn out and ragged clothing that Mother could not bring herself to send me to school. Warm clothing and felt boots were
lacking for the winter, as well as money for note books and text books.
Then help came in our need. My brother-in-law David offered to take me
in and get me completely ready and buy me books and notebooks. My
sister Tina wanted to sew me a school brief case.

But my mother could not reconcile herself to giving me up, especially
since she also calculated that my sister Tina would soon have a baby. She
did not want the young wife to have to burden herself for my care. But
David thought that I must go to school or there would be punishment from
the officials. So they agreed together on the following measures: David
and Tina would keep me from Monday to Saturday evening, and over
Sunday I would be with Mother.

At Tina's there was better food, and every day I received a piece of
bread spread with lard to take along to school. However, I did not eat it
but gave it to my brother Gerhard to take home to Mother.

On September 22, 1934, Tina gave birth to a little girl and named her
Freida. From then on, I did not feel so lonesome. I tended the baby in its
cradle and helped to take care of it. Two years later I came home completely to my Mother, because now things were going better for her and
she had enough to eat for us.

1936 was a year of good harvest. Her wage in the collective farm en-
abled my Mother to buy a cow. Only with our clothes was it still hard to
get everything in better shape. Out of old curtains, Mother sewed a
blouse for each of us youngest. Besides that, she was able to buy a black

porter's cloak. Anna now possessed one dress, and I even had two dresses, because I was going to school.

Afterwards we even got Sunday dresses, and we felt ourselves especially rich! From my sister Tina we both received a little red kerchief. Even though it was very small, we tied it on ourselves and thought we were most beautifully dressed.

In the spring, the cow lost her winter coat. We brushed the shedding hairs out and dropped them in hot water, so that they could better be pressed together, and make a ball. Finally a piece of material was sewed around this to make ready a grand play ball. From the rags that we could collect, we sewed doll clothes and out of clay we formed many a toy.

Often times we played at having a funeral. For that, we laid a tiny doll in a matchbox and carried it solemnly into the garden. There we made a hole and buried the tiny doll. On the next day, we hauled it out again, so that we could play with it further.

Through going with my school mates, many wishes awoke in me. My greatest wish was to have a leather briefcase. Naturally, I also wanted to have a rubber ball, that could bounce so beautifully, which was not possible with my home-made ball of cow's hair. My school friend also had rubber galoshes, while I always had to go to school in wooden clogs. I often came home with wet feet. For this reason I yearned for rubber galoshes! Then a neighbor lady said to me, "You can buy all these things for yourself when you are working and earn something."

We children went out working in the summer. The girls weeded the vegetables, while the boys helped weed the sunflower fields. They rode the horses that pulled some kind of a machine, and watched that it would pass exactly between the rows. We got very little wages, however, so that it never reached far enough for us to fulfill our wishes.

As time went on my mother acquired a sheep, a pig, and ten hens, besides the cow which she already owned. To be sure, we had to give to the collective farm the greatest part of the milk, the wool, the eggs and in addition 88 pounds of meat. But the rest helped our family to get along better. Now we had enough to eat, and could buy the most necessary clothing.

While our Mother and the older brothers and sisters worked in the collective farms, we two youngest, Anna and I, remained at home. We fed the young pig, hoed weeds in the garden and cooked the food, in the best way we could. Often we had potatoes baked in their jackets and barley grits. We were so proud when Mother and our siblings came home from work in the evening and we could set the prepared meal before them!

Often Anna and I hurried nearby to our grandparents to help them with picking berries, harvesting beans, hoeing weeds, or whatever was to be done. Our wages there were the privilege of eating until we were full. We were especially pleased with the beautiful stories that Grandma knew how to tell in such a lively way. During the summer, our Mother could not tell us any stories because she had to work from early to late on the collective farm. However, she made up for it in the winter by telling us stories and singing a lot with us.

The harvest of 1937 turned out better than that of the year before. As wages we received many watermelons, cabbages, pickles, and straw for the cow. My mother and my second oldest sister, Lena, had worked their fields so well that they received bonuses. Lena bought herself a guitar. Jakob had dried so much cow dung for winter fuel that he earned himself a mandolin. Gerhard got a balalaika and we two youngest together earned another guitar. From then on there was much music in the house.

We sang many beautiful folk songs. Spiritual songs we knew very little about since they were not sung in the schools. The strings on the little guitar often broke and substitute strings were hard to come by, so Gerhard used strings from the balalaika (which were easier to get).

Our cousin often came over to our house to play with us and sing. When we had harmonized enough, our Mother told Bible stories or read out of Christian books — those that had not yet been confiscated by house searchers. We children were especially deeply impressed by the Joseph stories. Our Mother tried also to give us children good instruction for living right but that did not please the young fellows and they took their jackets and caps and left.

When we little ones went to bed, Mother would tell us about the Savior Jesus Christ and pray with us. I was often worried about thinking of death and hell, but I wanted so much to go to heaven. I listened very quietly and reflected much afterwards. Anna, however, always had many questions — her mouth was never still.

In the Autumn of 1937, my sister Lena married Jakob Petkau. The wedding festivities took place in the school. The newly married pair were given a little room with other people , the rent of which they paid by helping provide heating material.

Chapter 3

The Poverty of the War Years

The following winter was especially hard. Since the administration building of the collective farm was across from us, we could always observe how calamity broke in our village. Almost daily an automobile of G P U (Secret Police) drove up. Then men were hauled out of the houses and into the auto. Most of them — including our Uncle Johann — disappeared forever in the icy regions of northern Siberia.

German background families were especially hard hit. With those remaining behind, great sadness and poverty reigned. All requests, pleas and attempts to seek mercy were rejected. There was no mercy.

In the summer of 1941, the war with Germany broke out. Then the misery for those from German background became greater. While they were not drafted for military service, almost all able German-descended men from 16 years of age on up were called up for forced labor.

At the beginning of 1942, there was a knock at midnight on our window. My two oldest brothers, Jakob (32) and Johann (19) had to make themselves ready immediately, to be taken away at 5:00 A.M. Mother quickly awakened both of them, and then also our other children. The necessaries in clothing, underwear, needles, thread, eating utensils, and coffee made from roasted rye grains, were all packed together.

Mother admonished my brothers, in all their needs to turn to their Redeemer, and said to them, "Who knows if we shall ever again meet on earth?" At 5:00 A.M. horsedrawn sleds arrived and my both brothers had to climb in. Altogether there were 63 men who were taken from our little village. At parting many tears flowed.

In March of 1942, the second group was taken and in October the third group — in the latter my youngest brother Gerhard (17) went along. My

Mother did not know how to equip the youngster with clothing, because she had already given everything usable to the older brothers. She had no shoes and no felt boots for Gerhard, only wooden clogs. She ran by night to people in the village but nobody could give her felt boots either in exchange for grain or as a loan — there were just no more to be found.

So Gerhard had to leave wearing, wooden clogs. Mother wrapped his feet with a covering because it was already very cold and snowing. With tears in his eyes he said farewell with these words, "Mama, we will never see each other here again." And that is how it turned out. Nobody ever learned what became of him! To all inquiries and questions the authorities gave no exact answer.

In November, 1942, came the order that also the women and girls from 16 years upwards would be drafted for forced labor. Only pregnant women and ladies with small children under 3 years of age dare remain home. There ensued heart-breaking farewell scenes. Mothers wept and cried, clasped their arms around their daughters and tried to hold them tight. But they were torn apart by violence.

For the collective farm work, only very old men and ladies with children were left. These ladies were trained as tractor drivers for the next spring and the old people had to care for the collective farm cattle — feed them, milk them, clean the stables, ect. The children fetched the straw from the straw-stacks in the field, on horses, on horse-drawn sleds.

For my mother this was a hard time. The water for the cattle had to be drawn from 80 feet deep wells of the neighbors and the feed for the animals had to be fetched from the field. In winter our little cottage was sunk in snow up to the roof. What work it was to shovel free the house door and a path to it! I could not go to school anymore, but had to help work. Meanwhile, I had become 15 years of age. With other girls in the summer I raked together the hay and later the straw and set it in piles. The 10 year old children loaded these piles up on ox-drawn wagons and built them into stacks on the steppes. Many times they wept from the tiredness and sank down, dead-tired in the evening in the camps.

The harvest production went backwards because the land could not be properly worked. Therefore food became scarce — but we still had to deliver to the government the same quota of grain as in the good years before. So nothing was left over for us. In order to try to satisfy their hunger, collective farm workers roasted wheat kernels at threshing time and ate them. When they went home in the evenings, they filled their pockets of their clothing with kernels of wheat and cooked them at home for food.

As a consequence of the hard work and bad nutrition, my Mother sickened badly. In addition came depressing bad news out of forced labor camps. Especially in the Molotoff Camp near Perm, where my youngest brother, Gerhard, was sent, frighteningly many men died. That unsettled and depressed my sick mother much. In her physical and spiritual need, she cried again to the Lord, that He would keep her alive for the sake of the youngest children. This time also she was heard and once again she recovered. The medical care was very bad. There were no medicines and you had to help yourself with home remedies, which the old people still knew about.

The letters that came from the forced laborers said they had to work hard, had little nutrition, and had bitter hunger. Their clothes were tattered and they never received replacements. Most of them had only what they wore on their bodies, so that they could not even change their wet clothing for dry. This led to bad illnesses and many deaths.

So the year 1944 arrived and there were renewed demands for the workforce. Once again 16 year old girls were taken to forced labor. I also got the order, together with a girl from a neighboring village and five young fellows. Mother was completely disconsolate and almost died from fear and sorrow, for I was not yet grown up, and so delicate and small and until now never away from my home village.

Great excitement reigned in our house, but all the wailing helped nothing — we just had to finally begin to get everything ready for the departure for forced labor, and start packing. During the whole winter I had been traveling back and forth fetching feed and straw for the collective farm, and my felt boots were worn out so I could not travel anywhere with them. In addition, it was January, and icy cold. Fortunately, I did not have to leave in such a hurry as my three brothers when they were drafted to forced labor. I had enough time; namely one day and one night!

My mother said, "With these boots you cannot travel. They will first have to be re-soled." I had already seen how my brothers had resoled their felt boots, and even helped them prepare the shoemaker's thread for the sewing on of the soles. So I took courage and began the difficult work. My mother still had enough gray thread, which she had traded from the Russians for grain.

I fastened this thread to a hook on the wall and doubled it until I had four long threads side by side. Then with Mother's help I twisted these treads together and rubbed them with cobbler's wax, making one heavy thread out of four light ones. Then the sewing could begin. With much difficulty we then were able to sew a new felt sole on the felt boots. The heels still had to be sewn on, otherwise the stockings would show. When all was done, I, considered my handiwork with pride.

Meanwhile, Mother was baking a "meal" with fourteen year old sister, Anna. She fetched everything nourishing that was left and put it in this cake. It contained a pouch full of barley grits, some flour from a sack, a little fat in an aluminum canister, and five smoked sausages. She packed in addition a padded comforter, a pillow, a jug, an enameled plate, writing paper and a pencil. Everything was stuck in one sack, full to the top. I tried to lift it up and carry it, but could not.

Mother became very sad again. How could her delicate girl ever carry this burden? Also my heart was heavy. Above all I feared the bitter cold and the snow storm which raged outside.

I put on all the clothes that I had. Even though I wore thick woolen stockings, my knees were freezing. So Mother fetched out the padded pants which I had always worn while bringing back the feed. They looked kind of strange because of the many mendings, but the ice cold wind and the snow forced me to put these pants on.

Towards midday, the sled came to our yard, to take me away. On the sled lay a heap of hay for the horses, because the way to the train station was about 62 miles. My sack was loaded up. Mother had prepared lunch for me, but I could not eat a bite. Tears ran down my cheeks, my heart beat fiercely from fear, and thoughts rose up in me. This is perhaps the last time that I will be together with Mother—no more words of comfort from her. No warming up any more at the oven, no more being at home! Dark clouds overshadowed my mood.

Mother also was very sad. She knew I would be coming into very hard living conditions. The letters of my three brothers and other young people from the village who were in forced labor, led us to fear the worst. How should I ever be able to hold out when I was still so little and delicate and already exhausted by the collective farm work from early to late. Tears stood in my Mother's eyes as she said, "Child, eat the warm soup! Perhaps this is the last time we shall be together. If we do not see one another again here, then we will hope that we shall see one another again up in the heaven with the Savior. When you are in danger or at the end, then cry out to God. Don't forget that!"

I became yet sadder. Would this really be the last time? Would I never see my home again? Then it was time to say farewell. I dressed while the tears were rolling over my face, and Mother acted as if a piece of her were being torn out. The driver called impatiently — "Quick! Quick!" I climbed onto the sled, the horses moved off, and the journey began. As long as I could still see Mother, I waved to her.

Chapter 4

Exile To Forced Labor

After two miles and a bit, we came to the neighboring village, where the district government was. There stood several more sleds, which had gathered up the young people from neighboring villages. Among them were my cousin Jakob Regier and a youth named David Heide. Some young girls were also there so that I would not have to be alone among strange young men. Probably I had never met these girls before, but that would soon be remedied (as we got acquainted).

At the government office, papers had to be filled out and that lasted some time. It was evening by the time each had his papers. The snowstorm had become stronger, so we young girls asked the officials if we could not spend the night at home. We were afraid to get lost in the snowstorm and perish. Next morning we could rise early and begin again. After a long time of discussion, the officials agreed that it was too dangerous to begin to travel 62 miles that night to the railroad station, so they allowed once more to go home and stay overnight.

My mother and my sister Anna had a joyful shock when I arrived unexpectedly at the door! They asked, "Don't you have to go afterall? Can you now stay at home?" But their joy was soon dampened when they learned that I only dared to stay for this night, because the snowstorm was too dangerous. We hung my wet clothes up to dry by the oven, and after much conversation we went to bed. I soon fell asleep in the warm bed, but Mother hardly closed her eyes, from sorrow over my fate.

Around 5:00 A.M. (it was still dark), they knocked on the window, "Maria, hurry up! We have to leave!" Quickly I dressed, said "Goodbye", and climbed on the sled next to the others. The village slowly disappeared from my view. I asked the others, "Shall we never again see our village?" This thought was very heavy for me.

The sled drove quickly away. It was cold and the wind blew snow in our faces. On the evening of the second day we stayed overnight in a Russian village. We laid down in the furs we had borrowed from home and were soon asleep on the floor. Early next morning, there were knocks at the door. An old man, who was already up and sitting at the table went and opened it. In streamed a crowd of school children and sang a Christmas song. It was January 6, 1944 — the day on which Russians celebrated Christmas by the old calendar. The old man gave a little gift to each child: a few pennies, a pencil or penholder.

More groups of children came into the room. They all sang a Christmas song and received gifts before leaving. For us girls-who were German — all this was new and interesting, for with us Christmas was celebrated differently.

After we had breakfast the journey continued. As night began, we had reached the town of Orenburg. We traveled to the quarters where a crowd of ladies and girls were waiting, who had also been drafted for forced labor. We had to now give our furs back to the driver, because they had only been lent to us. Then he turned us over to a guide who would bring us to the assembly place. We were twenty five persons. Three succeeded in fleeing. I would have liked to flee too, but could not because now the guide watched us more closely.

Now we went by foot to the railroad station. Since I could not carry my heavy sack, I remained standing. Then the guard was forced to carry my sack himself or send my cousin Jakob Regier or David Heide to help.

The train pulled into the station and everybody tumbled head over heels to climb on. Since the train only stopped for a short time, it left about half of us behind, including Erna, with whom I had meanwhile made myself acquainted, and me. The guard had his strong wish, to keep his little sheep together. He was afraid that in ensuing confusion another couple could run away. So he gave David the charge to watch over us.

The next train would only come two days later. But the transport of forced laborers could not wait so long. Then a freight train came along with open wagons. The guard spoke to some soldiers for permission to divide us up among the open cars so we could travel that way at least to the city of Busuluk, and there transfer to passenger cars. So that's the way we went. Standing on open freight cars traveling in 30° cold weather was frightful. The ice cold wind blew about our ears. We kept stamping our feet and beating our arms about us but the icy wind and the snowstorm would not be affected by that.

All at once the train went slower and we could now hear how the wheels of the locomotive slipped and turned and squealed in one place and another, the tracks were so full of drifted snow that finally the train had to remain standing. Now we were standing in a open field and there was no settlement to be seen anywhere near from which to fetch help. We were told that it was only a mile and a half to the next station. The locomotive was uncoupled and sent on ahead, to bring another locomotive to help.

We stood and froze and waited. But no locomotive came. Then one of the soldiers said, "It's only a mile and a half. Better get on the way otherwise you will freeze." One person was appointed to watch the baggage and the rest of us went on our way by foot. Hardly were we in the Busuluk station when the train came slowly in! Everybody ran to the freight cars to get their baggage.

But what a shock we got! My sack was now squashed half empty, Erna's suitcase had disappeared completely, and all the Russians had been treated the same way! Now a search was conducted of all the cars. The Russians cursed. The women cried and scolded. All the searching was in vain. Already the locomotive whistled and the train began to slowly move. Many were still searching the cars but had to now jump down, because the train was picking up speed. Then a couple of soldiers called out, "Hey there, here is your suitcase!" — and they threw it down to us.

It was Erna's suitcase! But she opened it, and it was empty! Only a writing tablet and a pencil still lay in it, apart from some scattered flour. Erna cried out loud. Meantime it became dark. We all sat in the railroad station and waited for the next train. Our hands were swollen from the hard freeze.

Finally the train came. Fortunately the compartments were warm. After a whole day and five hours of traveling, we arrived at the last station. We had to report, all of us, to the officials and were enrolled in lists and divided up to different quarters.

Erna and I could remain together. We received quarters with a woman and her 15 year old daughter. Inside it was agreeably warm, the way Russians love to have it. We set aside our snow soaked clothes to dry them. Then we went to unpacking. Erna was sad because she had almost nothing left. But I consoled her and said, "I still have a lot, and it belongs to both of us." We packed all our food provisions in Erna's suitcase. Then we ate until we were full. "You know what? Let's write a letter home now!" I said. Then we began to write the first letter of our lives.

Erna asked, "How does a person start? And what shall we write?" I replied, "I don't know how to do it myself. But at home we did receive a few letters from my brother, who was also in forced labor. I know exactly how he always began, — 'Good day to my much beloved Mama and all the brothers and sisters!' So we can do it the same way."

So we began, and then described how we traveled, what we had seen, how we had miserably frozen on the icy, open freight cars, then later had to go by foot, had our things stolen, and what kind of quarters we now had. We also wrote that we were homesick and longed to go home. Last of all we included greetings for all our loved ones, and asked for an answer soon. We stuck the letters in envelopes and waited to mail them. "Ach, my dear, there are no addresses on them yet!" said Erna. "And we have to still put our new return address on them, otherwise we can receive no answer." I agreed. Our landlady told us her address, and then we wrote it on the envelopes.

We carried the letters together to the next post box and rejoiced at the prospect of the soon answer. On the return journey, we thought it was now time to wash ourselves and get rid of any bugs we might have picked up on the trip. So we did that and were hardly fresh once again when my cousin Jakob Regier, with David Heide and Jakob Penner showed up. Shortly thereafter, Peter Derksen and Jakob Toeves came out of another neighborhood. All five told us of their lodgings, and that they also had already written a letter home.

Over and over again we spoke of home, what they were doing there, etc. Then the youths said goodbye and promised to come again. It was hard to have a conversation with our landlady and her daughter, Anasha, because they understood no German and we only a little Russian. Therefore we had to help make ourselves understood with many signs.

Then it was time to go to sleep. But where should I lay down? There were no beds. In the room stood only a chest, a table, a chair and along the wall a small bench made of boards. We asked our landlady, "Where shall we sleep, then?" She laughed and said, "There on top of the oven!"

"Oh, but where will you two sleep then?"

"Naturally, also on top of the oven!"

That seemed strange to us, to sleep on top of the oven, and besides, four people together. We had heard that the Russians slept on their ovens and that it was nice and warm up there. So there was nothing left to do but climb on top of the big wide oven. It really was nice and warm up there, and we soon went to sleep. But it did not last long before we woke up again because of the cockroaches and bedbugs crawling all over our hands and faces. It just swarmed with these bugs! That was just too awful for us! We packed up our sleeping things and lay down on the wooden floor boards. That remained our sleeping place as long as we roomed with that lady.

Chapter 5

Homesickness And Hunger

Early the next morning the brigadier or boss drummed us out of sleep. He took us about a mile from the village to a stone quarry. Here we received our tools which included wrecking bars, picks, long chisels, heavy sledge hammers, shovels, and spades. Then the word was, "Now! Get on with the work; in the evening I will check what you have done during the day." The Russians among us were not so energetic and said to the boss, "Nothing much can be done today anyway! Give us first the ration cards for bread and other food, and with that we will be able to work!"

"You will get those things soon! But now, never-the-less, you must start! We will set an overseer over you who will take care of finding enough cards for you!" answered the boss.

David Heide was set in as the overseer. "You are responsible for twenty two persons, that they fulfill their norms, that their tools are clean, and that nothing will be stolen," said the boss to David.

"Come with me, now, and I will give you the bread and ration cards for all of them. You cannot go to the dining room each time, because it is over two miles away and we will lose too much time with that. And now on to the work!"

"Good, good!" said the people. And the boss and David went away.

None of us had ever done such heavy work before, for this reason we were working as those who were quite unskilled. The wrecking bar was very heavy; many of us could hardly lift it. Picks we were seeing now for the first time. When we wanted to hack the stone loose with them, sprinklings of stones would spurt into our face and against our legs. None of us were able to break the larger stones the first day.

34

Such a day seemed terribly long to us! We always would look at the sun again to see if it wasn't ready to go down. Since we did not have any mid-day pause, we went home somewhat earlier; for to sit down under the open heaven, and on the ground in such cold was too dangerous — one could catch cold very quickly doing that. A barracks, in which one would be able to rest for a little bit, was nowhere to be seen.

David said, "Now we will make an end for today!" We were all just about frozen, and tired. "I've got the ration cards by me, so that you will not lose them, or anyone will steal them. Each day we will send two or three of you away, to fetch the bread and the rations."

Our rations for one month were written out to be eleven ounces of fat, twelve ounces of fish, nine ounces of sugar, about three pounds of flour, besides which we all received daily bread in the amount of twelve ounces per day. It was sour, strongly salted, and very wet, so that it would weigh more.

"What our mothers baked, tasted much better than this," we all said.

"When will we ever again be able to eat such good bread?"-"When the war is over and we come home, then we will all have good bread again," said Jakob Toeves.

"Who knows, when the war will ever be over! Maybe it will last so long that we will all be dead by that time!" said Erna.

"That's also possible," answered Peter. "Have you forgotten, what we found in the letters that came out of the Molotov Camp? That many have died there, — today this one, tomorrow that one." — "But now that's enough of that," interrupted Peter and put the conversation to a close. "The girl's hearts will be too heavy! Now what else? Give me first some money, so that I shall be able to buy some bread!"

We all paid up; I now still had only 210 rubles left (for which one could buy two and a half pounds of bread). Since it was now getting dark, we all went to our lodgings.

Our thoughts continually turned homewards. We sat down and wrote another letter to our loved ones because we were homesick. "Ach, if only we had an answer from Mama already," we said. Then we lay down to rest, and told stories about home, until our eyes closed for tiredness.

That January was bitter cold — and in addition we had only our bad clothing! How we rejoiced, when we were able to come home after work into the warm room! There we would cook something warm for ourselves and our spirits returned to life once again. After that Erna would sit by the window, look with homesickness out the window, and begin to sing; "In a distant land, far over the sea, in a city in America lived a mother with her child, very lonely there, still God was with them in his grace. The child often heard her mother sing of a land, that was in the heavens, where joy and fullness and loveliness would reign, and where one would be free of sorrow and burdens.''

I sat down beside Erna. Ardently we sang together this song of the homeland. While doing it the tears rolled over our cheeks. Sometimes we couldn't sing any further, because we were crying too hard. Our landlady heard our sobs and came to us: "You dear children, please don't cry so much! Because you could become sick from such heavy homesickness! Soon the day will come, in which you will be allowed to go back home again! — " "Ach, it's too far away!" sobbed we girls.

"Never mind, never mind, it's not that bad," said she.

"The time will come for you, when you can be leaving." So the old lady tried to console us homesick girls. Shortly after that when the three young men came to visit, the old lady told them how we had wept so bitterly from homesickness. Then the young men wanted to laugh at us, but Erna turned to them with these words, "You may have your good laugh. You are three together, that's why you are not so lonesome!"

"Well that's probably true," answered David, "But from crying nothing ever gets better. Let just the first three months go by, and you will have accustomed yourself to this, and you won't even want to go home anymore!"

"That you don't even believe yourself," I threw in, "you only want to tell us something! My homeland I will never forget, even when it becomes so good here."

One day I became sick. In my upper thigh I developed a large ulcer and had terrible pains. For two days long I tortured myself with it, then I could not go any further. What should I do now? I was ashamed to tell David but Erna reported to him the next day; "Maria cannot come to work, because she has a big ulcer and a high fever." Then David came and said, "You must go to the physician! Simply to remain at home is not allowed, or I will get into trouble! Ask your landlady where the nearest doctor is."

I was shy of going — especially if the doctor would be a man, — but overnight it became even worse. For this reason I got ready the next day and started on the way. The doctor, however, had gone away and with great difficulty I dragged myself back to the lodgings. This day was very long for me, because the pains incessantly tortured me. How glad I was, when Erna finally came home in the evening! On the next day I limped again to the doctor. There it went much better for me, than I had thought; the doctor gave me a salve and tablets and wrote me down as sick for a couple days. Finally the ulcers went away and the pus flowed out.

So that the time would not seem too long to me, I used to help the landlady with her work. We sawed wood together, split it, carried it into the shed and cleaned the room up. Her sixteen year old daughter went to school and the mother was employed as a night watch woman in the horse stables of the collective farm.

Since Erna and I still often cried together, the landlady proposed, that also the three youths would come and take up lodging with her. "Where shall they then sleep?" we asked. Then she pointed to a place where there were boards against the wall.

"But tomorrow they can't come, because we are celebrating 'Pominki' which is a special six weeks festival." Then she baked piroschki which were special confections made with white cabbage, potatoes, and onions. "This evening lay down on the oven, because many guests are coming to visit me," said she, and so we crawled up on the oven.

The landlady cleaned out the room, so that only a small table remained in the room. She placed candles on it, lit them, and laid a thick book beside them. On the wall she hung a large and beautiful icon, or religious picture.

Then a priest came in a black cloak and in the corner of the room sat a dark clothed lady in mourning. Many guests came in. The priest read something out of the book, and the mourning lady began to weep loudly and to cry out. That sounded terrible to us. The guests crossed themselves and bent down to the ground. Many times they knelt down and they bowed their heads to the floor. This celebration lasted a whole hour. Then the landlady acted as a hostess to her guests giving them the paroshky and tea. Erna and I had never seen such a celebration before. Then we could tell our young cousins many things and also write a long letter home again.

On the next evening came our young cousins. The landlady said to them, "I can't stand it anymore how these girls are always torturing themselves with homesickness. If they write a letter they begin to cry; if they sing a song they begin to cry; its all one here whether they are alone or not they begin to cry. So that will not go on any longer! It would be much better if you three would also live here." She pointed over to the boards along the wall. You can sleep over there, because it is warmer than along the floor where the girls are sleeping. The youths were agreed and brought their luggage. They could also speak Russian well and sing, and that pleased the lady very much.

After I had become healthy again I had to go back to work. Besides that, we helped our landlady often with the sawing and splitting of the wood, so that she would be able to keep our apartment well; otherwise we would have been much colder, since we slept on the floor.

One evening when we came home from work, our landlady was almost beside herself with great joy. "The cow has calved! A beautiful calf!" said she.

In the first days the cow gave milk richly, so that even we got a mugful. It tasted splendid. After that, however, the milk hardly was enough, just for the little calf. The cow was too lean, and could simply not give more milk. Outside was frigid; therefore, our landlady brought the little calf into the room. She prepared him a space with straw and strewed ashes all round it, so that the urine would not run out into the rest of the room. As soon as the landlady noticed during the day, that the little calf wanted to make his business, she would hold a pan under him. But during the night of course that didn't work; so this liquid ran across the room many times to our night sleeping place. Everything became wet, and that was really not pleasant. How should we dry out our bed things after that? But it became even worse! One day the landlady brought the cow inside the room to milk it. It was just simply too cold in the shed outside in which the cow usually stood. What kind of a mess that produced is indescribable. It stank terribly and the old landlady cursed and scolded. We had never even heard of such a thing up to this point!

She was upset by a new discovery of bad news: our rations seemed to be disappearing. That could not really be allowed to keep on happening! At first we held our landlady in suspicion, but we never saw her cooking any grits, like we had. She prepared her meal out of crushed oatmeal. She secretly stole this when she was the night-watch woman in the horse stall. Could it be that the young men were quiet participators in this deed? It seemed to us that they did not go around sparingly with their rations, and cook the same grits like I had brought with me from home. They could not steal from the old landlady, for she herself had nothing. I wrapped up my last 210 rubles in a handkerchief, laid it in the millet pouch, bound it up and marked it exactly with knots in the rubber band and the position of the pouch in the suitcase. Then I shut the suitcase, and went to work. In the evening my first look at the suitcase seemed to show everything alright. It was locked but inside things were just not quite right: the rubber band and the knots were differently placed. And of the grits, only half were still there and the worst — the 210 rubles were gone! That was a hard blow and I was inconsolable. When the young men came home, they hypocritically gave expression to their sympathy and bewailed this bad luck with moving words. But later I found out that one of them had actually been the thief. I took the last grits and cooked them and Erna and I ate everything up together.

The work in the stone quarry was always more difficult, and we just did not seem able to fulfill the quota. One day, when some of us had been sent back again to fetch bread, we came back with empty hands. The baker had baked nothing, because the bake ovens were broken. Without the daily bread ration, it was hard to work, if not impossible. Since our own provision's supplies were used by this time, Jakob Regier was looking in the little house of a lady who was not yet at home for something edible and found two thick onions. He stole them and said, "So now at least we having something to eat!"

I still had a little bit of salt and some parched corn coffee. So I fetched it along, too, and we sat down at the table, cutting the onions into pieces, dunking them in salt, and took them with a teaspoon of the corn coffee and swallowed it down with a swallow of water. "This meal I will never forget for my whole lifetime," said I. "Ach, if only my mother knew about this!"

In our desperate situation Jakob said suddenly, "Do you know what! We should run away from here!"

"How would we be able to do that?" I cried. "We would never be able to find the right way home!"

"You let that be my worry," said Jakob. "I am your cousin and I will take you along. David will take Erna with him, and the other young men can go together. Then it will not be so difficult if we go only two at a time!"

The thought of going home again awaked in us girls a cheerful hope but we really didn't trust ourselves completely to the matter. Would the young men perhaps leave us stuck somewhere? I expressed this doubt, but Jacob passed it off.

They could never treat us so shabbily.

"But now enough talking about that; it's gone too far," said Jacob then, "We would rather sing because we haven't done that for a long time. So then we sang youth songs, and suddenly the young men began to sing

Russian songs which they had also learned. They sounded so heavy and sad and sorrowful, that all of us had tears running down our cheeks. The landlady heard our singing, came in and said, "You will all die from mere sorrow! Lay down and sleep. It is already very late."

Life became even harder. The young men took our cooking utensils and traded them for just a few potatoes. That was our last nutrition there. Things looked just as bad with the whole work group. Because of that most of the Russian ladies and girls had already run away. Only seven Germans and a few Russians were still there. David and Jakob tried once more to get bread, but they were unsuccessful. So we starved further. We wanted to wait still for seven days, until bread would come again. We hoped then after the bread had been delivered, that we could begin our flight. We didn't even go to work anymore. Nobody came to check on the work. The work brigades which were nearer to the office complained much to the officials and therefore they still got their bread. But our brigade could not accomplish anything because we had a German brigade officer.

The seventh day dawned. It was the first of March 1944 — and Peter said, "This makes no sense to wait any longer. Whoever wants to can wait on death, but not me, I've had enough. Whoever wants to come with me can come! I'm going while I'm still able to go. If I have to die then it's all equal to me whether I die of hunger here or under way. If it is to be, we will succeed in getting home and if not, then everything is over!"

David answered, "I think so too. Look to it whoever of you wants to save his life! Here there is nothing more to hope for. But I'll have to go last with Jakob, because as the brigadier leader, or officer, I can't be missing; otherwise there will be a lot of trouble, and everything will go to pieces. Perhaps I can turn it around so that they don't notice anything until all of us are gone; otherwise they will quickly catch each of you!" Then we girls were restless; we couldn't go away alone, how should we begin that? We didn't know either paths, nor the way. "You won't leave us to stick will you?" said we.

But my cousin David spoke up quickly, "In no case! We have promised you. But we still have to be the last to leave. You go with the other three young men before us."

"That'll never work," I said, "They are already a threesome together, and we just won't fit in with them!" Therefore David spoke with Peter, that he should, besides the other two young men, take us two girls with them. After a long time of talking about the matter Peter was agreed with this.

"Alright, I'll do that! I already have one such trip behind me and I've seen a lot and lived a lot. Just come with me!"

Then we took counsel how long it would be before we would start, which way we should strike out on and how we should move and do things. We had to reckon with a ten days' march by foot. "Alright now get some sleep! Tomorrow morning early at 5:00 by the first light we are going away! First we will have to make two miles and a half to Pochwist and have that behind us; otherwise the officials will know right away, what kind of birds we are! By the time it's brighter, we will be able to have reached the next village." Could we trust these young men? Would they still leave us stick? For a long time we girls did not go to sleep.

Later we found out the truth: Jacob and David had made other plans for themselves. They would break away and remain only so long as they would be able to get bread for the whole brigade, and rations and supplies also for the days that were behind us. What they did not need for themselves, they were planning to sell, in order to buy tickets, or if no tickets were to be bought, then they could use the money to pay the fines if they would be caught on the trains.

Chapter 6

Flight In A Snowstorm

Next morning while it was still dark we got up and got ready. We did not want to take much with us. I packed in just a spool of thread and my cup in order to have something to barter for food. I even took the pillowcase off, and tied it around my neck, because it was so cold. I pulled on my old quilted trousers that had been darned over and over again, and the quilted jacket, too. My blankets I surrendered to David and Jakob that they might sell and give me the money later but I actually never received it. Erna took her own light covers with her. She wanted to trade them herself for edibles.

Jacob and David accompanied us to the door, and wished us luck on our flight. Outside the three other young men came to us. Unobtrusively we succeeded in reaching the next village and there we immediately sold Erna's blankets for five hundred rubles. We divided the money evenly among us so that each one received one hundred rubles. That was actually not much because one could only buy six hundred grams of bread for it. Five of us as a group would not dare to remain together long. Peter suggested that the three young men should go on ahead about a kilometer. So that they would still always be in our vision, and we two girls would come along after them. It was thirty kilometers to the next village, and there is where we wanted to stay overnight. That would be enough for the first day. Otherwise we would not even be able to go further on the next day, in case the snow storm held up. Furthermore, we were hungry and weak.

These were great exertions that we were letting ourselves in for. But the thought of going home always gave us new courage. "Oh, if only the snowstorm would stop," I groaned. "It makes it so hard to get ahead, because it is continually in front of us, and we are already so tired! And one day isn't even over yet!"

In the evening we reached the village and saw that the young men went into one house, but then immediately came again. It was the same thing with the second house. But by the third house they had luck — they did not come out again. Erna said, "We will go over to the other side and ask there. — "But you must ask," said I, "Because you know Russian better." We went into the next house, gave polite greetings, and Erna asked if we would be able to stay here overnight. In that home there was a woman with two children. She considered us both for a while, and then said, "Yes!" It was as though a stone was lifted from our hearts, that we finally had some good luck. The housewife asked us to take off our wet clothes, and to put aside our felt boots. "And now you can lay down on top of the oven where you can really get warmed up." We didn't need to be told that twice. Oh, it was so nice and warm up on the oven! The housewife wanted to ask many questions and learn much from us, but we were both asleep in a moment.

After a time the housewife woke us up and said, "Come girls! Eat a little bit! I see that you have not had anything to eat. I myself don't have much, but what I have I will give to you. I know how much hunger hurts!"

She set before us a plate of boiled potatoes in their jackets, a little bit of salt, and then brought us, as a good neighbor, a glass of thick milk. To be sure bread was lacking, but we were cheerful and thankful that finally we were able to get something into our stomachs. We thanked her over and over again. Talked about many things, and then laid down on top of the oven where we blissfully fell asleep.

Early in the morning we got up. The housewife gave us still more potatoes and salt for breakfast, and then some more of them to take with us on our further journey. She accepted nothing for our overnight stay and food. So kind and sympathetic was she. With hearts full of thankfulness we took our leave of her. Outside we met the young men. They had gotten nothing to eat so we gave them the potatoes the woman had given us.

It was fifteen kilometers to the next village. There we sought to beg some nourishment. But the people there had nothing themselves; their children went around pale, hungry and in tatters and rags. They wandered about, or sat in a corner. Even the adults were very badly clothed. The only grub that we could rustle up was a little bit of bloated pumpkin and a potato.

By evening we were again looking for lodging. At one house they wanted to turn the dogs on us, and at another house the cry was: "Go to the community officials and they will give you some lodging if everything is alright with you. But if it is not, then you must be runaways. And such people we cannot keep overnight. Out! Get away with you!"

Downcast we went from there—thoroughly chilled, with wet clothing, and hungry. We were met by a lady coming back from getting water and we asked her about getting lodging for the night.

"That'll never work, because you will freeze with me. I have no wood. For the whole week long already I haven't been able to heat the house. I lay on top the oven with two quilts but that still doesn't help. And for you, I have nothing."

With that we despaired of begging and pleading; "Where shall we go then?" We just can't stay outside in this kind of cold!"

"At my house it is cold as well."

"Yes, but inside at your house this frightful snowstorm isn't blowing! We would even pay for the overnight lodging!" Finally the old lady softened, and took us home with her.

She only had a very little earth house. And what poverty reigned inside! The very small table, and a little chest,—that was all the furniture. Otherwise there was nothing at all. The walls glistened with ice. When you would speak, your breath turned into a white fog. "Do you know of anyone that could sell us a kilo of potatoes?" we asked. "We have such a hunger!" The lady went outside and shortly came back with a kilo of potatoes. She fetched a little wood to cook the potatoes, but the wood was so wet and made a lot of smoke, so she had to open the door, and the bitter cold rushed in. After we had eaten we laid down in our wet clothes on the floor. We shivered from the cold and our teeth chattered incessantly. It was impossible to sleep! The night seemed to be endless to us. Our bodies hurt, but less from the hard floor, then from the freezing and shivering. Finally it became light. Each of us gave the lady ten rubles, and then we went on our way.

Outside again in the storm we only really felt how much our limbs hurt. Snow flurries had become thicker. I complained, "I'm only sixteen years old, but I've hardly ever had anything good. I hardly even knew my father. And, how I always longed for father! From little on up I was hungry and I have seen only poverty. Mother was often sick, we had no help. For a time we lived with our Uncle Jacob. How he cared for his family! At Christmas each child received a little something. But we didn't even have a little piece of bread. At that time I was three years old. How it hurt Mother when we children begged for a piece of bread! When we were bigger and things were going a little better for us, we were suddenly scattered in all directions, and now I have to live through something like this. Is this going to be the whole story of our youth?!" Heartbrokenly we both began to weep.

Just then a sled came passing by in which two men with yellow shoulder tabs sat. We were immediately afraid that we would be stopped and arrested. But fortunately they drove on. How we breathed a sigh of relief! "Our greatest wish was still that no one would report us or point us out!"

Now it had become evening again. Once again we had to seek a night's lodging, and knew that with doing this it would be easy to be picked up. But it couldn't be helped; to stay out in the snowstorm was impossible. At the first house we were turned away. Then we went up to a very poor looking house. Because the poor have suffered themselves, and have experienced pain, they are more likely to have sympathy. This is what our mother always told us. A poorly dressed woman came to the door, and Erna said, "We seek a lodging for the night. Please don't turn us away." And actually the lady did invite us in. And how beautifully warm it was inside. At the table sat a man, and we were immediately afraid of him. But the lady set before us some thick milk, potatoes and a "Lepjoscha" cake and asked us to begin eating. The cake was bitter to be sure, because the wheat had been ground into flour with all kinds of weeds. But when a person is so starved, then even such bitter things taste sweet. We felt ourselves fortunate. Then the man began to question us out: "Where have you come from? Where are you going?"

In the fear that he would report us, we didn't tell the truth. We said that we were on the way from Kujbyschew to Busuluk and our tractor had broken down. We had wanted to buy some milk, and to see if we could come back and get it another day. It was true that a tractor had traveled through this way. But of course, we did not belong to it. The man gazed at us and said, "That doesn't sound right. Probably you have run away from somewhere!" Then we blushed right up to our eyes, and were silent. We were both ashamed and frightened. But he said then, "You don't have to have any fear of me! I, myself, have a daughter who has gone through forced labor. I know what you are suffering!" Then we confessed everything to him. We were overcome with sleepiness. The man also noticed this. He heard that in this day we had walked thirty kilometers through storm and snowdrifts to reach this point. We didn't have to be told twice to lay down, and we were soon fast asleep.

On the next morning we got up by sunrise. The woman gave us some breakfast, and the man described for us the way ahead. Full of thankfulness, we took leave of them. We were cheerful and encouraged that we had found a warm corner and something to eat. But then a new kind of worry crept up on us: How will it go today? Will we at all ever reach our goals? Many times we prayed; for our mothers had taught us how to pray. We could not understand how God had led us on such difficult ways. Yet, we still had an unwillingness to do unjust or wicked things and to grieve God. As it became mid-day, there another village lay before us. "Now there we will have to beg something to eat," said Erna. "Perhaps someone will give us something."

During the first days of our flight, begging was always very hard for us to do. Whenever we tried to do it our knees started to tremble. Little by little, however, it became easier. Often we experienced rejection; many times we remained hungry a whole day.

Now we came to a house and begged for just a little bit of a warm reception. "Just come in here," said the lady. "There are already three young men here who are hungry." What a joy we experienced in seeing our familiar acquaintances. The lady had put on a kettle with small cooked potatoes and salt. We peeled the potatoes, sprinkled the salt on them, and ate. That tasted so good. With hearty thanks we went our way again. Peter said to us, "It will be a long way before we reach the next village. We shall have to hurry. If we arrive there too late, we will find no lodging. In that village the local officials as well as the county officials have their headquarters. There we may very easily be arrested. Inquire only at little poor houses. If it goes well, by tomorrow noon we should be in Busuluk."

What fatigue! Our feet would hardly go any further and the storm had still not ceased. We turned our faces aside, but the wind threw so much snow into our eyelids that we could hardly see anymore. We could not keep up this pace much longer. For four long days we had been underway and gone about thirty kilometers each day — now we were exhausted. The young men were so far ahead of us, that we could hardly see them anymore. Now it became dark again. In the distance we saw little lights. The district capital already had electric lights, which at that time was seldom seen. After three more hours we finally arrived there. In between we watched almost all the light go out. But one house we knocked on the window. "What do you want so late?" asked somebody.

"Just to stay overnight!" answered Erna.

"Not with us. Go to the officials. They will test your papers, and decide who you are. Move along with you now!"

Sorrowfully we went further on our way. All at once Erna called out, "There in front of us is still one light. Come quickly before it goes out!" We knocked on a window, and a lady asked, "Who is there?"

Erna called, "Alas, dear lady, please let us stay overnight with you. We have been in a snowstorm the whole day long. We are tired and frozen."

"No, that will never do! I have a big family, and in addition have taken guests already."

We pled, "Please have pity on us. We would gladly just lay down on the floor. But we do not dare stay our in the storm anymore. Please! Please!"

"No! That will never do! The room is full from one end to the other. Go to the neighbor's house. She often takes someone in overnight. Perhaps she will let you come in, too."

"But over there it's dark, she is already asleep." "Well wake her up then! I cannot help you even with the best intentions." We went to the neighbor lady and knocked. Full of fury she came to the window: "Who are you disturbing us so late. Get on with you! Get away! Go to the officials!" And she went away from the window.

What now? Erna suggested: "Let's go back to the first lady now, she at least has spoken with us a little. Perhaps she is a little bothered by our plight afterall. So we returned and knocked again and said, "The neighbor lady will not take us in. Won't you have pity on us! We can't stay outside!" The lady seemed to be arguing with herself for a time, it almost looked as though she was going to have mercy on us. But then she said, "It just will never do!" And she turned her light out. There we stood and did not know where to go. The frost crept into our bodies. We trembled. Then a thought came to me: "Today is Saturday, outside of many houses are saunas which were surely heated up today. If the saunas were open, that would be a place we could stay until morning. Then we left and made our way quietly along. "But unfortunately the doors of the saunas were locked, too. "There is still the cowstall!" said Erna, "Maybe its open!" The first door was locked, but the second was only latched. We opened it and looked inside. We noticed that a cow lay there. She was not tied, and immediately sprang up. "Don't let her out! Then the people will notice and report us at once to the Police. Then we will really be in trouble," said Erna. You hold the door shut, afterwards I will hold it shut, and we will do this taking turns. We won't be able to sleep, but at least here there is no storm blowing."

We looked around for a dry place, but there was none there. The stall was too little — actually only so big that the cow could turn itself around.

Our felt boots were thoroughly soaked, and it was too filthy in the stall. Beside the cow there was a very small place where we could sit down with our feet drawn under us, and warm ourselves from the cow. Suddenly we heard somebody whistling, and steps came into the barnyard. We thought: "If they only wouldn't come into the stall!" Finally the whistling ceased and the steps went back into the house. Then we began to breathe again. Why did this night seem so long! Again and again we peeked out to see if it would not soon be dawn. Finally it got brighter. Quickly we went out, locked the door behind us, and got away from there.

On the road everything was still quiet, no human being was to be seen or heard. It was icy cold and we beat our arms about us, but that didn't help. Then we saw a lady with two big buckets, who was going to fetch water. We asked her about the way to Busuluk. She gave directions to us, and thankfully we went further. In the next village we tried to beg some food. We got a little bit of watery pumpkin an ate it greedily up.

From another house we received a piece of raw potato as big as an egg. Shortly after that we met up again with the three young men. Even they had spent a bad night. Peter pressed for us to quickly separate from one another again. Otherwise, we would fall into greater danger of being arrested. He advised us here in the village to beg as much as we possibly could, because when we would come into the city of Busuluk we would not be able to beg. There in that city we should go at once into the first street to the left where there was a market. There we would meet and council further. From Busuluk we could then make our way further towards Orenburg.

Chapter 7

Obstacles To The Journey Home

Towards midday we girls arrived in the city of Busuluk. Right away we found the street and the market, but nothing was to be seen of the young men. The market was much bigger than we had thought, and now it happened that Erna and I lost each other. There was so much to see—provisions, flour, grits, potatoes, pumpkins, items of clothing and the many people who rushed here and there. By just for a moment looking elsewhere, my friend was no longer to be seen! Now I really became afraid. What could I begin to do if I could not find Erna anymore? But suddenly I saw my friend again and called to her, "Let's get out of here as quickly as possible, otherwise we are really going to lose one another!"

We left the market place and stood together in a side street by a fence. "We're already five days underway, I am already exhausted, and we still have five days before us," I complained. "How shall we ever do it? I can't keep it up!" With that I began to sob heavily. Erna consoled me— "There, everything will go better! We just can't keep standing here. I'll tell you what. We'll go to the railroad station and catch a train." On the way we asked a lady when the next train left for Orenburg. She said, "It's already gone, but this evening at seven another one leaves!" Since the police kept appearing and checking peoples' permits, we made ourselves scarce and went back to the market. We stuck close together, so we would not be separated again. Everywhere we asked about the prices, and took little samples of flour and grits with our fingertips, to see if they tasted bitter. Finally we bartered a spool of thread, which I still had with me for a little something to eat. Burning with hunger, we gobbled the food.

It was evening. We didn't dare go into the train station without having tickets. We stayed outside and nibbled on raw potatoes. One lady came up to us and asked, "Wherever did you buy an apple?" — "Oh, that's just a potato," we said. Why ever are you eating it raw? And where do you want to go anyway?" — "We're going to Orenburg," answered Erna. At that we became very shy and looked suspiciously around. But because the woman seemed trustworthy to us we told her everything. "In that case I advise you don't travel by passenger train. Here in the station everything is strictly controlled. Already many have been arrested. Look there they are coming again!" With that she pointed to two policeman, who went about scrutinizing the people. "Better set yourself on a coalcar, or a freight flatcar. They're not so strictly controlled."

The lady went away and soon the awaited train appeared. Crowds of people rushed into the compartments and thereby made a great noise. They pushed and shoved — it was a miracle everybody got in without someone being trampled down. We girls gave up trying to get in, and let that train go. "Now we have waited a whole day in vain!" we moaned. But the very next train which is coming now we'll have to take. It doesn't matter what happens after that, because we just can't hold out anymore."

Finally we heard a train coming nearer, but then it rushed on past. A second and a third one did the same. Exhausted and freezing we spent the night in the open. We had no permits and were afraid we would be arrested. What we would have most loved to do, was to hide somewhere and go to sleep. But we were afraid even of that, lest we should never wake up again. We had often heard of people being frozen to death that way.

Towards morning it became perceptibly colder. Then we saw in the wall of the guest house a steam vent with hot steam coming out of it. We crept close to it and there warmed ourselves so that our clothes thawed out again. Afterwards we tried to walk on, but were frightened, because our clothes froze stiff, and we stood there as if we were carved out of wood. We were miserable enough to die. Once again we began to weep bitterly but there was no one there to comfort us. Still one thought came to us — "There is one who will not abandon us!" We knew that at home our mothers were praying for us without ceasing, and many times it seemed to us as though we were surrounded by these prayers. "When we get to Orenburg everything will be better," said Erna. "My mother lies there in a hospital. Let's go there, perhaps we'll get something to eat there." Over and over again our thoughts were about eating and about resting somewhere warm.

We often stopped in toilets, because we did not feel the horrible wind there. The night just seemed to never end, but finally it became day. "Oh, if only the passenger train would come! I can hardly stand up, or go any further from exhaustion," said I. "Here in this station there are too many watchers. If only we were away from here!" In the railroad station waiting room we kept looking at the clock. It seemed to always be another two hours until the arrival of the train, so impatient was our waiting on it. We wanted to wait on the other side of the tracks, and there board the train. We vowed that we would never let ourselves be parted, no matter what happened. And if one of us would be captured, then the other one should allow herself to also be captured, so that we would always be able to stay together until the end. After a long time the train arrived. We rejoiced with an indescribable joy, but at the same time our hearts beat heavily from anxiety, wondering if we would succeed.

With a big jolt the train came to a stop. We crept quickly under one of the cars and out on the other side. "When the locomotive begins to whistle we will place ourselves on the boarding step, when it whistles three times, then we will know that the train is ready to leave," said Erna. When it whistled, four Russian girls sprang ahead of us onto the boarding step, then Erna and I followed. The train moved slowly out and we six girls held on. We soon began to pass in front of a group of men. One of them sprang up to us and tried to pull me down. Probably because he heard that I had spoken German. He scolded and shouted, "Get down here you fascists! Because of you I have suffered much in the war and almost lost my life. My brothers are still at the front. Get down with you pests! I'll pull you down! You will not travel with this train!" He pulled at me but Erna and the other girls held me securely from above. The man ran screaming and shouting beside the train. The speed picked up, then the other men shouted, "Let her alone! Otherwise both of you are going to fall under the train and be squashed!" Furiously he let loose of me, clenching his fists and shouted something which we could not understand anymore. "That was lucky that he didn't succeed in pulling you off! But I would have jumped right down after you, no matter what it would have cost us." My knees were trembling from excitement. I could hardly stand, and my heart beat so loud that I could feel it in my neck.

We traveled on into the night. The wind blew strongly, and we were almost freezing, because we stood on the windy side. The Russian girls experienced the same thing, but they could stand it better because they were not so exhausted and hungry as we were; besides they had dry clothes on. We had to hold on with both hands, if we didn't want to fall off, because the train jerked powerfully many times. Already I had no more feeling in my hands, and the trip on this train would last eighteen hours, until the next morning. Could we hold out so long? Our wet felt boots froze fast to the boarding step, and only with extreme exertion could we loosen them from it. Then we placed ourselves in the doors between the two cars, because the wind there was not so strong. Erna just now realized, that her mother was not in Orenburg but in Pokrowka, in the hospital. At the next train stop she asked a conductor how many stations it would be to that point. "Still two," she got for an answer. At the next station we jumped down, in order to reassure ourselves that this information was correct. The official there told us, "Well you have just traveled past that stop!" That was a pity, but now there was no way to change it.

Then the coach door opened, and two officials came out to check our tickets. This was a main control-point, at which the chief was present himself. "What kind of little rabbits are these?" said one of them, "What are you doing here, and where do you want to go?" He fetched us into the coach, and also the four Russian girls. "So now show me your tickets!" "We have none!" "Well, then you are going to have to pay ninety-five rubles fine, and at the next station you'll have to get out!" The Russian girls paid at once because they had money, but we had none. Some people were standing in the coach who also had no tickets. There was a big confusion. The conductor gave orders: "Whoever has already paid shall stand on the left side, and on the other side the rest of you can stand!" We placed ourselves on the left side with the people who had already paid. Shortly thereafter the train stopped, and many more people pressed in. After that there was such a confusion, that the conductor soon lost sight of the illegal travelers. So the two of us came out of that one.

The lady porter looked at us. She was not so dangerous, she said to us, "At the next station you must get off, otherwise you're going to end up in prison!" Once again, short of our goal we had to get off in the cold, or do something else. So we hid ourselves among the travelers until the train left. The lady porter discovered us there, "But I told you that you had to get off!" "Oh please, please let us travel to the next station anyway," we pleaded with her. "We'll hide ourselves in the toilets so we don't take anybody's place." "No that'll never work," said she, "The toilets will be locked by the officials. Pretty soon the next stopping place is coming, then do nothing but get off!" she commanded, and disappeared hurriedly into the coach. What to do? "Here it is so beautifully warm I just don't want to think about going out into the ice cold weather. I'm staying here," confided Erna. So the two of us remained inside, even though we were full of fears.

At Orenburg we fled from the train. At the barricade stood two policemen, who were checking passports and tickets. There was a great crush because so many people had gotten off. The police grabbed one or another but it was not possible to check everyone, because the big crowd of people kept pushing and shoving from behind. We girls pushed ourselves back in order to get through the barricade as quickly as possible without being checked. I almost had a misfortune because one of the policeman grabbed me by a fold in my jacket and pulled me to himself. But with a mighty pull I tore out of his grasp. The policeman then grabbed another person who was carrying two suitcases and pulled him to the side. We were so glad that we had escaped this danger! Now we wanted only to get away from the railroad station as soon as possible!

We hurried into the street and asked the lady there for Kobsowa Street, which led to our collective farm district. All of the necessary clothing, building materials and so forth had to be hauled by horses from the city to our collective farm. We hoped to find one of these horse-drawn sleds that could take us home again. Soon we came to a court-yard where we saw a sled standing and Erna met there an acquaintance of hers from our village. She asked him if he could take the both of us. He had already loaded the horse-drawn sled, with tractor parts, among other things. His horse was somewhat weak, and for this reason he did not know if he would succeed in getting home with such heavy cargo. He proposed to us: "Go with me on foot beside the sled; I can only travel by foot myself. In the next village about twenty-five kilometers away we will probably meet another cargo sled. It will be carrying gasoline and oil. Maybe there you can hitch a ride." We were agreed with this simply because no other possibility seemed likely.

Soon after we met five other girls who had also fled from forced labor and had been at Orsk. Three of them came from my own village. All five girls wanted to join Erna now. The hostess heard our conversation and said, "I will quickly cook you up a soup. Then you can lay down for a nap, until the man is ready to travel."

How wonderful that seemed to us—a warm room, and a hot soup! The lady gave each of us a pair of furs, saying, "Lie down now here on the floor and get a good sleep! You're probably cold clear through and exhausted from such a long journey!" We pulled off our felt boots in order to dry them on the oven. I couldn't get them off my feet because my feet were too badly swollen; so the others helped to pull on them until the boots finally came off. We folded ourselves up in the fur, and the warmth of the room did its work so that we were soon asleep.

After a few hours of deep sleep we were awakened, and got up. The way to the sleds didn't seem long to us for we had much to tell one another of the hard work, the flight and the fears we met underway. After a few hours we reached a mountain and saw the village of Kargala. From here it would only be two kilometers more.

All at once we saw seven sleds coming from the direction of our home. What a joy it would be to us when we would once again be able to see the people from our village! And so it actually was! Among them was my cousin Heinrich Regier and my cousin H. Esau.

We presented ourselves to the headquarters. There the men unpacked their food and invited us to eat with them. My cousin laid something before me and said; "Now, eat until you are satisfied!" But an older man warned me: "Don't do that, that could be your death, for you probably have not eaten bread for a long time. How long has it been since you began traveling?" I reflected and said, "Fifteen days!" — "Well if that is so, what have you been eating in that long time? How have you possibly still remained alive!" Then we explained what experiences we had. We didn't eat too much, even though we had a great desire to do so. How good it felt in our stomachs! We felt ourselves almost lucky.

Since there were exactly seven large sleds, each one of the sleds took one of us girls. Whenever it went up hill, we climbed off because the horses were not very strong. Seventy-four kilometers still lay before us. Cousin Heinrich took me on his sled and said smiling, "How Aunt Tina will be happy when I bring her Maria back again!"

By dark we came into the next village. The horses were unharnessed and fed, and we went into warm quarters. But hardly had we sat down when a rider came with the news that we should come home immediately because Uncle Heide and Uncle Regier, who were with us, had a summons to appear before the village officials. They discussed this news back and forth and came to the conclusion: "If we all immediately travel on, then you girls will also be right there. Then when they know that you have come, you will all likely be arrested at once. So for this reason Uncle Heide, and Uncle Regier decided to travel home again immediately and not to mention a single word about us girls. Meanwhile we should dawdle a little bit on the way, and stay overnight somewhere else. Perhaps in this way we run-aways from forced labor could enjoy a few days at home before we would be captured and sent back again. Thus we found ourselves not yet at home, and already afraid that we would be shipped back to this inhuman forced labor!

On the next day our journey went further. Oftentimes we had to get out and help push the sleds because the horses did not have enough strength. Sometimes the horses lay down in the snow and nothing could make them move until they had rested. After they had rested for a time we were able to help them get up again with our united strength pulling them to their feet. One pulled on the tail, another lifted against the side, and another pulled on the head. When the horse finally stood up, it was trembling in its whole body. Unfortunately the feed was used up, otherwise the animals would have something with which to strengthen themselves.

During the last kilometer we girls often tried to stretch and look ahead to see if we couldn't see any of our friends. To be sure we did see some acquaintances, but none of our relatives. It was not known, as yet that we were coming home. The men had kept their word and told nobody about us. Our little house right at the beginning of the village was locked and snow reached to the window in the gable. One could see that a short time before some snow had been shoveled away from the door, but now once again new snow was lying in front of it. From the roof to the street one could only see a steep and high snowdrift. Our mother out of deep poverty was not able to eat much, and for this reason had gone to live with my sister Helena. This sister did not have to go into forced labor, because she still had two small children under three years; but her husband was also drafted to the forced labor in 1942.

A little bit further on I saw my younger sister Anna, who was playing on a sled with her friends. When Anna recognized me, she jumped up and ran over to greet me very emotionally. We wept, and then we hurried home to Mother. My sister Helena came, too, with her children, Tina and Jascha. They were all shocked at how thin I had become. "Now you are only skin and bones," they said.

At midday they had a meat soup since they had recently slaughtered a sheep. With great satisfaction and almost greedily I ate two plates full as well as a piece of bread with it. I would have gladly eaten more, but Mother was afraid to give me more. Couldn't I even eat in my own home until I was full? But Mother said, "It has happened in the past that somebody that ate too much became quickly very sick, when they were as starved as you are. You don't want that to happen, do you?" No, of course

I didn't want that to happen. But my raging hunger was too great, since I had hardly had even a little piece of bread up to that point; but only some milk and a few potatoes, and some pumpkin. Mother consoled me, "In a few hours we will cook some potatoes for the evening meal. Then you can eat some more."

My sister's children then brought me some carrots and biscuits, which were baked out of flour and ground sugar beets, but my mother warned the children not to give me any more lest it hurt me. After the evening meal my friends came to visit me. But when they saw that I was exhausted and sleepy, they soon left. I lay down to rest, and slept immediately. However my sleep did not last long. I woke up because in my stomach and my intestines, I was frightfully upset and had gas and pains. Many times it seemed to be as though my body would burst. I tossed and turned here and there until the morning dawned. Now I understood why my mother had warned me not to eat too much.

Chapter 8

Hard Experiences In The Forced Labor Camps At Orsk

On the next day was the funeral of one of my cousins, and I attended. Many acquaintences were gathered there and expressed alarm over my appearance. They thought of their own relatives who had also been drafted to forced labor; many of them had tears in their eyes at the thought.

On the third day I went along to help do some clean-up work in the village. On the 13th of March, 1944, a big barn with many cows and calves had burned down. Forty nine animals, a third of the herd, could not be saved, and perished miserably in the flames. They looked frightful as we dragged them out of the ashes. The animals were skinned and cut into pieces and the flesh was sold. Some people had no money to buy any, so they came with knives, took off the fur, and ate from it the half baked flesh, in order to fill their stomachs. My brother-in-law Jacob who also had run away from forced labor shortly before and I, carried in a bucket whatever meat we could including some calf tongues.

I had hoped that I would be allowed to stay at home and work. But on the ninth day there was a knocking on my window. I was ordered at once to report to the village officials! With that my short time of freedom was at an end. About twenty persons came together, all of whom had fled, even Erna was there. With a heavy heart I took leave of my mother again. She could see with her own eyes how terrible thin I had become. With one guard who would accompany us to a new collection point, our sled journey began at ten o'clock in the morning to take us to the railroad station. From there we went to the city of Orenburg. In the train Erna and I unpacked some edibles to strengthen ourselves, "Just look at what our guard is eating!" He had white bread and butter smeared on it, and in addition, a honey comb. "Such a thing I have not even seen in one of my dreams, much less tasted! That probably really tastes good!"

At the Orsk Station he had to deliver most of us including Erna and me. In this place there were some thousand women, old and young from all directions under heaven, all of them sentenced. Erna and I were shown to a barracks where a hundred and thirty women lived in one room. As we found out later, in every crack of the two story wood beds uncountable bugs sat. Soon we also felt how troops of lice crept around in our clothes and tormented us unceasingly.

On the next morning we were driven to work. We had to break up earth-works with wrecking bars, chisels, picks and sledge hammers. The earth was frozen rock-hard and very difficult to break up. Since I was one of the youngest, I was set to work in a roofed-over hall. There large blocks were manufactured out of slag, cement, chalk and clay. I pushed the blocks away with a hand cart, or brought them with a lorey to dry in the hot air of a heater. I also had to carry and push the blocks in a wheelbarrel, for two persons, to the place where they were heaped up. I often had to carry and shove the heavy stones all myself. Each one weighed about 50 lbs. Sometimes I stood beside the pressing machines and carried the still wet blocks down. That was hard work for me. But who cared about that? The daily norms had to be fulfilled! If I did not fill my quota of work, then I would have to work longer than the twelve-hour work day until enough was accomplished. It was always shouted at us: "Quick! Quick! and Forward!"

The bread ration consisted of seven hundred grams daily. The bread was wet and salty. One could easily press it into a ball; and one did not become satisfied from eating it, to do such heavy work in the cold. So physical weakness began to grow. Many times we bought a quarter liter of machine oil and dipped the bread in it. Many also secretly stole the oil, which was strictly forbidden. One eighteen year old youth by the name of Shultz worked at the motor of the block press, and secretly sold the motor oil to the people in order to get money to buy himself more bread. He dipped the bread in the motor oil and tried to gorge himself on it. But from that he got a terrible diarrhea and the oil completely soaked up his clothing.

One morning I went to the dining hall and wanted to fetch my bread. There was a youth who during the night peeled potatoes and with that could finally eat enough to make himself satisfied. He found some oat grits and ate and ate until he couldn't eat anymore. Then he went out. Scarcely was he away from the door when his stomach rebelled and all the grits came out again. I saw how good food splashed out on the ground. In that same moment a man came by who could hardly walk from weakness. He saw how the young man was vomiting the grits. With both hands he swept them up from the floor and ate them with a fierce hunger. In normal times he would have been disgusted by such an act.

How bad it also was with our clothing the following circumstances show. Many women, myself included, received bedclothes, and even a straw sack, a bed cover, a pillowcase, and a towel. Up to this time we had to sleep on the bare boards of the bunkbeds. Our clothing was completely torn and ripped. And for this reason we now used the bedclothes to make ourselves clothing. Among us was an old lady named Petkau, who was very skilled in tailoring clothes. She cut up the pieces and we sewed for ourselves what clothing we could. So that it would not be discovered, and also that we would not have to wash so often, we dyed these clothing pieces in dark colors. Some women brought their bed clothes to the market and bartered it there for edible provisions. They wanted just once to eat enough to be satisfied. So once more they were sleeping on the bare boards, and were covering themselves only with their felt jackets.

Every ten days we were driven to the bath house. This happened at night so that no work time would be lost. Again and again some tried to hide themselves from going to the bath house, because they were dead tired and would rather have slept. They hid themselves as well as they could but the overseer who accompanied us to the bath searched everything out, even the toilets, so that nobody could hang back. It often happened that just then another brigade was at the bath house, or waited for their clothes which had been given over for delousing. Then one or the other had to wait half the night until they finally came to their place in line for a bath. But then they were still so endlessly tired!

When finally the bathroom was free, we went inside. At the door stood a lady and smeared each person's hands with a teaspoonful of soft soap. That's what we were supposed to use to wash ourselves with. Many however were so exhausted, that they could not wash themselves, but cowered down in a corner and slept as long as they could until the words came to awaken: "Get up! Fetch your clothes, because they are now being given out!" The delousing was often very badly done and the women mocked: "The lice are now just about warmed up enough that they can more quickly jump from one person's clothing to another. They would just love to try another post!"

Once one of the girls hid herself under the boards and the overseer did not discover her. While the rest of us were taking time in the bath, she slept so deeply and soundly, that she did not even notice that a rat was chewing on her big toe. Only in the morning did she find out when it was too late, that her toe was eaten off.

As a result of the weakness and malnutrition, for many of these women their monthly periods did not appear for three or four entire years. They were so worn out that many were despondent and had no more hope that they would ever come out of this misery.

In the year 1946 a frightful occasion oppressed the inhabitants of the Orsk Labor Camp. On the first and second of May and with the celebration of the October Revolution it happened that one Sunday was included with the Holidays. Then we had three free days. A young man with German background asked for permission to see his parents who lived in the vicinity. But permission was denied him. Nevertheless, he left without permission and said to the others, "I'll come right back, and in time." but he delayed getting back for a few hours after the three-day celebration was terminated. The Russian Commander was furious! He locked him overnight in a cellar and commanded the chief guard in no wise to let him out, even if he would scream ever so much. All at once the young man began to scream in a most miserable way. It made the night watchman very sorry to hear him and he would have gladly released him but he had too much fear of the Commander. The screams and cries became ever more horrible. After a time, though, everything was still. On the next morning they found of the young man only his ribs, bones, clothes and shoes. Now an investigation was begun to see what had eaten up the young man. A dog was poisoned and thrown into the same cellar. On the next day they found there three hundred rats. These rates had eaten the young man alive! Do you suppose the Commander has ever been called to give account for this yet?

With many of us, also with me, our bodies became quite swollen. And especially the legs became very thick. But no one had pity on us. The cry was always: "Forward! Forward!" It was completely useless to go to the doctor. He seldom helped, but usually sent the sick ones right back to work. We all had the strong impression that the authorities wanted to use up all of the Germans and bring them to their graves. How often I had to think about my house, and my family at home. To be sure my mother was poor, but she still had a little garden in which she could grow a few potatoes, sugar beets, red beets, and onions, and harvest them. How gladly I would have welcomed the opportunity to eat a fresh beet, but I could only dream about it! But one thing always gave me consolation and new strength to hold out: the knowledge that my mother was daily praying for me. Once in a while a letter came from her. That was the only joy in this hard discouraging life. I also wrote letters to my loved ones at home. Since I had no writing paper, I used, like the others, the gray inner lining paper of empty cement sacks.

Even those who stayed at home had, in that doleful time, nothing about which to laugh. My mother was required, like all the rest of them to maintain one cow, two sheep, and ten hens. How she was supposed to bring the livestock through the winter, nobody cared. Out of the garden she had to produce one hundred kilograms, from the cow two hundred liters of milk, or the equivalent of cream, from the sheep fifteen hundred grams of wool and a few liters of milk, and from the chickens one hundred eggs as well as forty kilograms of meat. The real estate tax for our house yearly came to 400 rubles.

My cousin Tina and I slept together, and also read our letters together. One letter from home brought the news that Tina's brother had died. Tina loved him so much and she wept heartbrokenly. But to travel home for funerals was not allowed.

Another frightful thing was that almost all the ladies and girls, because of weakness and malnutrition, were from time to time completely confused in their thinking. Tina and I were often seized by this, too.

On May 9, 1945,—I had been by this time already more than year in hard labor—came the good news: "The war is over!" This produced shouting and crying like you can hardly imagine. From all corners it rang out: "Hooray, hooray, now we are going home!" Most of us cried for joy; some even laughed—but there were very few that did that, for almost all of our laughter had passed away. However we were soon bitterly let down. The Commander (she was also a German) admonished us, "Don't think everything is going to happen so quickly. You'll never go so quickly! Until all the papers are made out, things will go on as they are; surely a few months, because there are so many of us here." But even these few months (so called) became years. Most did not get home until March, 1956, eleven years after the war.

To celebrate the end of the war, everyone was invited to the dining room for breakfast. Such a thing happened only very seldom. We just weren't used to things like this. Sometimes when a brigade had done very good work, we were rewarded for a few days each morning with a spoonful of thin, cooked grits in a plate. Now in the morning of the 9th of May, everyone received a heaped up spoon of mashed potatoes. And a spoon of liverwurst as well. The rejoicing that this caused is hard to describe. At noon we were treated with a fish soup, and a spoonful of grits. In the evening we received another treat: a spoonful of brewed potatoes and liverwurst. Everyone felt indescribably well and thought; "If only we would always get such good food then we could afford the energy to do the work." But on the following day it was like always. But hope that we could soon return home stayed with us. Still, month after month went by and nothing happened. Suddenly a few women who still had small children at home, and some that were ailing and half dead were allowed to go home.

Chapter 9

Sickness and God's Speaking

In the year 1946, we were given our first furloughs. Unfortunately it was strictly forbidden to travel home. Whoever would try it would be locked into a cell to sleep on the cold cement floor and receiving only 200 grams of bread and fish soup daily. Like five other girls in my brigade, I also received furlough, and we planned, despite the prohibition to try to travel home. We knew it would be very difficult, because the commander, whose name was Boschlakow, was very strict. He often disguised himself as an old lady, concealing his face with a headcloth, and creeping like a crippled person with a cane around the railroad station in order to observe all the people who waited for trains. The Germans were easy to recognize because of their bad clothing, their different behavior, as well as their speech. Whoever he caught was immediately arrested.

But why should we wait in the camp all those fourteen days of the furlough? That seemed to us to be inhuman. Since we had no money, we would have to take the railway by the black market (traveling without tickets). We familiarized ourselves with the train schedules and then went on our way to the five kilometer distant railroad station. It was winter and a snowstorm blew in our faces. At the railroad station we looked around, in case the feared Boschlakow might be there somewhere. We hid ourselves in the neighborhood of the railroad station. There it was made known to us that the train had been delayed three hours. Outside it was too cold, so we dared to creep into the station, in continual anxiety that the commander would come upon us. Everytime the door opened we drew back and thought, "Now he is coming!" After the three hours had passed it was announced that the train was still delayed another two hours. So our anxieties seemed to have no end. Finally it became light outside, the train crawled in, and everyone rushed out to the railroad platform. I was pushed and shoved by the crowds of people right up to the door of the train; but while the others climbed in, I fell in a faint, and remained lying there. Snow blew into my face, and then I came to myself again; but the train left without me. A few people were still in the railroad station. I crept inside and sat down on a bench. From cold and excitement and weakness my whole body trembled. After that I did not want to go back into the camp, but tried to reach my cousin who lived in Krekin five kilometers away. There I had to go to bed at once, and immediately fell asleep. I had a high fever and began to have fantasies. My cousin called the commander's wife to me, who ordered an ambulance to take me to the hospital. My fever was measured to be 41°C.

The lady physician immediately cut off all the hair on my head, because she diagnosed me as having head typhus. I was now as bald as a shorn sheep. But I rejoiced that each morning and evening I could enjoy a big spoonful of grits or potato soup, and at midday even another plate of soup in addition. It seemed to me as if I were in a sanitarium. I recuperated as the fever went away, and after twelve days I was released. I would gladly have stayed longer in the hospital because it was so pleasant for me there. Two days later I wanted to go back to work, but then a friendly lady from my brigade told me that I should report to the office that my whole furlough had been spent in the hospital. Possibly I would receive a substitute furlough. As a matter of fact, I did receive another twelve days to rest up. After that I came to the hospital for a few additional days because of a fall on my back. This was really not unpleasant for me. In the meantime I had driven the homeward journey out of my thoughts. All the other girls who had actually tried the journey had been caught and locked up.

Since the food never seemed to fill us, the workers always tried to round up something extra. For example, they often begged for the kind of beets that were raised for cattle feed and loaded on passing trucks. But with this you had to watch out, if you got anything, that it would not be taken away by someone else. One day I came home and saw how a girl from my barracks, who had an armful of beets which she was trying to carry home, was attacked by a fourteen-year-old boy. He threw himself on her and took her beets away. The girl cried loud, "Maria help me!" I hurried to help her, and picked up some of the beets which had been flung to the ground. Then another man jumped at me, gave me a blow on my lower jaw that threw me to the ground, and took everything away from

. My jaw hurt for a long time whenever I chewed anything. It often
ne to pass that stronger youths would fall upon the girls and women
d rob them. They were especially looking for foodstuffs or bread ration
kets.

Once in the late autumn, I came with my brigade about one o'clock in
e morning on our way back to the barracks from the late shift. We
ssed a certain courtyard, where a great pile of white cabbages lay. In a
le guard house the guard sat with a gun at the window; he had put his
nds up against his face and fallen asleep. When we noticed this, we
ept very softly up to the pile of white cabbages and each one took as
any as he could carry. The watchman noticed nothing.

Back in the barracks we thawed out the cabbage heads on a hot plate.
any did not even bother with this, but ate the cabbage frozen like it was.
eces of ice were falling from the leaves. Some held the cabbage in the
e in order to thaw it out. In our whole barracks this caused a terrible
or. But that meant nothing to us; the main thing was that we at last had
mething substantial between our teeth. The girls and women of the
her shift were still asleep. But now they woke up and noticed what was
ppening. Thereupon they quickly sprang up, dressed themselves and
rried out in order to profit from such a find. But meanwhile the watch-
an woke up. He saw that the white cabbage was being stolen, tore him-
lf out of his guardhouse and shot. One woman fell to the ground badly
ounded. She was taken to the hospital where she soon died. Some of the
omen were recognized and they locked them for a whole night long in-
de an ice cold cellar.

The commander's wife received the order to release four women work-
s to bury the woman who had been shot. The sister-in-law of the dead
oman and I were part of the group of four. We had no desire to take part,
it we did not dare to object. For work tools we took along spades and
gging bars, and a truck drove us to the hospital. A nurse at the hospital
ided us into the morgue, opened the door and said, "There she lies,
ke her out yourself!" In the cellar lay many dead persons and we were
orrified by them. We could not be moved to go down there. The sister-
-law begged us to help her, but we could not overcome our fear. Then
e sister-in-law began to cry and begged the nurse for help. For compen-
tion she promised her a coat, which she would actually take off the dead
rson as well as a pair of stockings. Thereupon the nurse called on oth-
s to help, and they laid the corpse in the coffin.

"Since we have another corpse, that of an old man who has no rela-

tives, let's put him in the same coffin with this woman. The coffin is big
enough. We could actually put five such skinny people into it!" said the
nurse. But this the sister-in-law refused to do; this was just too much for
her. We dragged the coffin to the truck in the courtyard and drove with it
to the cemetery. On the trip we sat on the coffin. The driver drove so crazily that the corpse in the coffin, which lay only on some boards, was
thrown here and there. We could hear the banging and clattering in the
coffin. At the cemetery we lifted the coffin down, and the driver drove
immediately away. Now we tried to shovel out a grave. It was so shallow,
however, that the coffin stuck halfway out. for this reason we tried to dig
deeper but the ground was frozen so hard that it was in vain. There was
nothing else to do than place the coffin in the shallow grave. The earth
lying around the grave did not suffice to cover the coffin. So we shoveled
some snow over it. "In spring this coffin is going to float when the time for
thawing comes," said one of the ladies. We sang a mourning song after
the burial and then began our homeward journey. In compensation for
this unpleasant work, we did not need to go back to work on the following
shift.

A single theme constantly moved us ladies and girls: "When will we
ever get back home?" It was promised to us for a long time, but the promises were not kept. Our courage sank and we no longer believed in the
promises that someday we would be free again. "We're going to die in
this misery!" said many. All of this still did not seem to be enough to
cause these workers in their need to turn to God. Only a few prayed (they
had learned it at home) but the main goal of their prayers was that they
could just once really have enough to eat until they were satisfied. Higher
goals they did not have, which one could understand.

Some days two bearded old Russian men came from a village about two
kilometers away from the camp and they told us about the Savior, Jesus
Christ. Several of the workers wanted to hear them and gathered themselves in their house. The men told Bible stories, prayed with them, and
taught them also some beautiful songs to sing. For example "My God
How Great Thou Art" and "Longing Day and Night." These women always wanted to hear more of God and Jesus Christ. They took other
women with them and soon the room was not big enough. Many more
grasped that Jesus lives, and is indeed our Savior. For this reason they
became cheerful and happy as never before in their lives. Now they could
even bear the miseries of the camp more easily. After the room became
too small, they prayed that the Lord might give them a larger room. And

as a matter of fact, one lady offered to give them her house for the services. They cleared out the few pieces of furniture, placed a little table up front, and simple board benches along the wall so that the old and the weak could sit down. It did not take very long before this room also became too small. Shoulder to shoulder the people stood filling the room right up to the door. So many came that some had to stand outside and look in through the windows. Even though they had worked the whole day long with hard physical labor, and most of them did not have enough to eat, they still gathered together with a great longing, to hear God's Word. Even if the service lasted two hours and they had to stand all this time, they enjoyed it.

I was not attracted to this. Only if I was invited by others, did I go along sometimes. Most of the time I found something in the services that I could criticize. One such song was the song which said, "Oh let not the spirit flee from thee. When will you do it? Why not today?" When this song was sung, I took it to mean me personally, but it did not suit at all. Other times they sang another song: "Standing before the door of my heart, knocking, begging: let me in! Do you hear Jesus' voice pleading?: 'Let your heart be my temple! I will make my dwelling with thee. Bring peace into thy heart.' Therefore don't delay, wake up! Believe, because it is not any joke."

At the end of each verse a solo voice sang softly but penetratingly: "Sinner listen!" I became angry about this, because I thought they were singing it only for me. I did not want to be counted as a sinner. For this reason I did not attend these services, which were being conducted in German and Russian, for a long time. But others pressed me saying, "Go with us again!" Finally I did go again. The room was filled to the door. Everyone tried to pull a little bit further back so that there would be room for me to get in, too. In one corner I found a place. The preacher was holding an earnest discourse concerning the second coming of Christ. He was saying that if one was not ready, then one must remain behind, and that would be terrible. Upon saying this he pointed with his finger in my corner and said, "Perhaps you there in the corner! If you have not yet accepted the Savior, then be converted today! Think on the end of all things, and on the Lord's judgment day! Come to the Savior, come yet today! Don't let the day of grace pass away from you." I got angry again and thought: "Someone has gone and told that preacher that I am here again today. And he was just talking to me personally!"

On that evening many who had made decisions for Christ remained behind. But I went to my barracks just the same as I had come, and I thought to myself, "I will still come, but only when I want to. Nobody has to talk to me about this. And indeed why should I need to be converted? I am not that bad! My mother taught me to pray, and I live a decent life! More than that is not necessary!" When the others in my barracks sang the new songs, I sang along with them. I fabricated for myself a notebook out of the gray paper of the empty cement sacks and wrote the songs down. But more than this I did not need to do. Or so I thought.

In the spring there was a flood water. Three other girls and I went one Sunday morning down the path, in order to see the flooded district. On our journey we climbed up a hill. Everything was completely still, the sun shone in a friendly manner and we four entertained one another long and loud, with stories of what had happened to us in the meetings. As we returned to the highway we caught sight of preacher Voth, who had the earnest discourse and had pointed with his finger to me. He greeted us with these words, "A beautiful good morning to you!" But we four were like mutes. Then said the preacher, "Just be true to your convictions. Surely you are also coming to the meetings tonight?" We denied this because we wanted to go up the mountain and look down over the flood. He took leave of us while we went further with blushing faces. "He probably heard our conversation. And now he will tell everything in the meeting," we thought. Thereupon we decided never to return.

Chapter 10

Hard Work, Home Leave
And Imprisonment

After some time I was transferred to the brick factory which was five kilometers away from Nikel. Nine months long I worked there. It was hard labor, and effected me very much. The accommodations were very bad. Fifty of us women were housed in an old sauna. We seldom got wood for heating. Therefore we had to steal our own wood. And therefore, we were sometimes caught. This was the only way we could have any warmth. Most of the time it was so cold in our accommodations that the walls glistened with ice. Only in the spring, when it got warmer outside, did the ice on the walls begin slowly to melt.

Unfortunately the bakery broke down in the winter of 1946 and 1947 and for three days we received no bread. Often it became black in front of our eyes, and some fell down from weakness. On the third day it was possible for us to steal some wood again; now we sat around the hearth warming ourselves. We had decided not to go to work. Now we were worried what would happen because of it. Hardly had we expressed our anxiety when there was a loud knock at the door. On our "Come in!" our supervisor rushed in, one who every morning had to mark the lists of who appeared for work. Without a greeting she screamed at us, "Why didn't you come to work? You criminals! The whole factory has come to halt because of you! You'll not get out of this one so easy! You'll all be put in prison!" We wanted to justify ourselves, but the supervisor did not let us say a word. When she had to stop for breath, we called out, "Give us bread , then we will work." Then she began to scream again, "Get out of here!" Get to work!" With that she grabbed a girl by the name of Anna Kirsch by the arm and tried to drag her out. At that we all got up and there was a wild screaming. The supervisor—who was a Jewess by the name of

69

Sophia Davidoff—screamed, "You Fascists, you Fritzes, you Hitler crowd! They should have shot you all! You are gobbling our bread and setting yourselves against us and won't even work!"

With the expressions "Fascists, Hitler Pack, and Fritzes" we Germans were often cursed. But what could we do, that Hitler had caused war against Russia and persecuted the Jews? Our forefathers had already lived for hundreds of years in Russia and had nothing against the Jews, but as German descendants, we were without rights, were oppressed and punished for the crimes of others.

We said to the supervisor, "We are too weak, we cannot work!" Then she ran outside screaming, "I'll fetch the chief!" It was not long before she came back with an official. Calmly he asked, "Why aren't you going to work?" Then the supervisor began screaming again. The official calmed her. At his renewed question all the women tried at once to explain about our needs. Then he called out, "Stop! Stop! That'll never work! When you all speak at once I can not understand a word!" One Kathryn Dyck began to speak, because she was more fluent in Russian. "Comrade T.B., we are now for the third day without a crumb of bread. We had to sell our ration cards, in order to get even a little bit of bread. And now we have nothing at all! We have no more strength to work. And just look at our accommodations here. The walls are glistening with ice! But we get no wood. And if we chop up some empty boxes, we are threatened. Nobody cares for us. And now Sophia Davidoff comes in screaming at us, pushes us around and curses us for Fritzes, Fascists, and Hitler Pack! Are we responsible for the war? Have we not worked well until we couldn't work any more?" And then she began to sob and all the rest of us began to cry, too. After we were once again calm, the official said, "Yes, you're right, how could you work under these conditions! You've only gone about it in the wrong way. You should have gone out to your work place, sat down there, and then said, 'We will not lift a finger, until we receive bread!' But now you have committed a group mutiny, for which you legally could all be locked up!" How we rejoiced to find somebody with whom we could speak reasonably! The official investigated our accomodations and found out that not even a toilet was available. For that, all we had were big casks to use which lay outside our building, and had once been used to make saurkraut. In the nighttime it was often so much below zero that if one went out to use such a "toilet" you could become seriously ill.

To conclude, the official ordered us all up and out and we went to the work place and sat down there to wait until we should receive bread. And he ordered the supervisor to apologize to all of us in his presence. This she did also but apparently it was very difficult for her. But from then on she was more approachable by us Germans.

Now we women began to work only the second shift from two o'clock in the afternoon on. The first shift was taken by German prisoners of war. When they came in trucks from their camp five kilometers away, they were singing their songs from their homeland. As they passed us German women and girls this made the tears run down our cheeks. But for us to speak with any prisoners of war was strictly forbidden and severely punished.

In February of 1947, some of us were transferred to the brick factory at Orenburg, among them myself. I rejoiced at being appreciably nearer my home. Our papers were stamped and each one of us received three days provisions in bread and one salted herring for the journey. At the railroad station we were packed into a cattle car. First our luggage was thrown up into the car, then some men climbed up into the car and pulled up the women and girls, because there were no steps to get in. There were so many people that there was hardly any room — we sat side by side on the floor. I had put my suitcase between my knees before I climbed in and in spite of that someone pulled it out and tried to make off with it. Fortunately someone noticed this and cried out, "Who does this suitcase belong to? It's going to be stolen!" So I got my luggage again. But my cousin's suitcase was stolen and never seen again.

Soon after that the train was set in motion and we all began to eat, even the bread and salted herring for the next day. That was not good because soon a burning thirst set in. But there were no toilets in the cattle car and the journey lasted thirteen hours. Underway nothing was opened up so that nobody would be able to escape. The next morning at 8 o'clock the train arrived in Orenburg. We all pounded on the cattlecar doors and screamed for water and toilets. When the supervisor opened up, many jumped out and began to go to the toilet whether anybody was looking or not. Then we were driven to our quarters in the city. Since we now had no more bread, we had to buy sunflower seeds from which the oil had been pressed out, a food usually given to cattle.

Later we were shown the whole brick factory, which had closed down for the winter. The next task before us was to clean everything up so that by the first of April the actual brick work could be begun again.

I worked together with Susanna Pries. She one day made a proposal that we should make an attempt to get a few days of unpaid furlough from

the director. We would try to travel home in order to fetch food supplies so
that we would be able to work better. With our hearts beating heavily we
went up to the director. He read our petition and smiled. Then he said,
"But you cannot go home now. It is thawing and the way the roads are
covered with mud, the autos cannot travel, and even the horses cannot be
used." Then Susanna answered that we could go as far as Platoffka, and
from there we had only another six kilometers to walk. This was not actually right, for Susanna still had another 45 kilometers, I another 76 kilometers to go. Since we had not seen our relatives for some years, the
director gave us six days furlough.

As fast as we could we hurried into the barracks, made ourselves ready
for the journey and went to the railroad station. The train brought us to
Platoffka, where we stayed overnight in a collective farm. Early on the
next day we set out on the way. A Russian man and a girl joined us on the
journey. The sticky earth clung to our shoes, so that oftentimes we could
not go further without cleaning the mud off our shoes. As often as we
could, we went on the side of the path. By midday we sat down at a straw-
stack and ate our bread. After a short rest pause we set out on our journey
again. Soon we came to a little stream, where the bridge had been washed
away. The Russian warned us about wading through the water because
there could be deep holes in the ground or even pieces of ice in the water,
and that could be very dangerous. We went on to another crossing, and
finally we had only one kilometer more to Susanna's village. Once again
a stream blocked our way; but this time it was not as deep as the other
one. We could see through the clear water to the ground underneath. We
waded through, and naturally got wet shoes and stockings.

Susanna's mother greeted us warmly and provided us with a place to
stay. Since we already had forty-five kilometers behind us, it was no wonder that we fell asleep almost at once. Unfortunately I had forgotten to dry
my shoes and stockings. So the next day I had to travel on in wet things.

It was Easter morning and the sun shone agreeably warm. Even if my
feet hurt, still the joy of seeing my loved ones once again gave me renewed
courage. Once again I came to a wide stream. While I was wondering
what I should do next, a ten year old boy set out from the other shore in a
feed trough, and rowed it over for me. Fearfully I stepped into the trough,
sat down, and the boy rowed me safely to the other side. Then he even
accompanied me for a little bit to show me the way. The road went uphill
and down until finally I saw my home village before me. Since my mother's house was boarded up, I turned my steps to the house of my sister

Helen. How great was the joy of my sister and brothers to see me again. My mother, who was participating in an Easter celebration, was fetched. And now my joy was complete. Since the roads were impassable because of the thawing weather, it was not possible for me to return six days later as I had planned. So I waited until the roads were passable once again. That was not until seventeen days had passed. Susanna had the same experience. We excused ourselves to the director, explaining how things had gone and the director accepted our excuses.

Back at work I had to shovel clay into lorries which was really hard labor. But since I had brought food provisions from home, I did not feel as weak as formerly. However, after three months I fell sick with malaria. Since the medical treatment didn't help me any, I secretly went back home in the hope that perhaps my mother would have a home remedy to help me. An acquaintance gave us the counsel to try the yellow blossoms of the sunflower plant. Since these were in bloom then, the blossoms were put in a glass of gin and soaked in the sun for as long as it took to turn the liquid as yellow as a tea. From this resulting tincture Mother gave me a teaspoon to drink three times a day. And as a matter of fact after a few days the fever attacks ceased and never came again.

After my recovery I stayed at home and went to work with sister Anna at the collective farm. After some time two young men came to me and reported that the police were looking for me. They tried to arrest my sister Anna, but a man from the administration showed them the mistake and cleared up the matter.

"Now would be the time for you to disappear," said the young men. But I went home, and on that same evening I was arrested. The next morning, the first of February, 1948, I was shipped away with nine other deserters. Because of snow storms and the weak horses, most of the time we had to get off the sleds and go by foot. In the County Seat we were locked into jail cells, four at a time. The so-called beds were unfortunately bare boards and we had nothing to cover ourselves except our padded jackets. It was almost impossible to sleep because countless lice and bedbugs tortured us.

In one corner of our cell stood a pail which was to serve as our toilet, and this was emptied only once a day. For this reason a fearful smell dominated the whole cell. Through one tiny window high up on the wall one could see a little bit of the sky. In the door itself was an opening which could be locked and through which our food was handed in to us. After fourteen days I was condemned to three months work camp and transported once more to Orenburg. There I had to help prepare food for 210 people-breakfast, lunch and supper. Over a two hundred meter distance I had to carry boiled water in heavy 10 liter buckets hanging from a yoke. To be sure, twice a day I had to carry thirty-six full buckets like this. Beside that I had to wash up the floors.

Fortunately, I did not have to stay long there; after nine days I was brought back to the punishment camp in Orsk. There I worked off the rest of my sentence. With a hundred other women-Russian, German, Kirgiz, etc. — together with all of them I lived in a large earthen hut. At the beginning I did not even know where to put my bundle of belongings. On the evening of the first day, as the many women pushed back into this barrack, Maria Reimer, Maria Schwartz and I stood at the entrance and had to wait until everyone was in their own place. There was not even a corner left for us so we had to put our few things on the floor in front of the hearth directly behind the unprotected opening through which the ice cold wind came. For covers we had only our clothing which we wore on our body. That was a bitter and hard time for us. But at least we regularly received three times a day, a ladle of oat grits and at midday a little bit of thin soup.

One day we were called out and marched by fours into a certain room. There I saw on one side visitors were standing, including my brother-in-law, David Petkau, who held something for me in his hand. After the identification, we were led by guards to where our relatives could bring us whatever they had for us. At a time like this the criminal prisoners who never received anything, always watched us closely, so as to take from us by force what was not freely given. My brother-in-law had brought me three jars of millet grits, a piece of bread, and a small piece of liver sausage. The grits I put in a store room for safety, and the bread and liver sausage I divided at once with an acquaintance of mine named Mrs. Enns, who came from my village. Then a criminal came up to me and said, "I saw it, that you got something. Give it to me, or else!" With this she spread two fingers and held them under my eyes. That meant: "If you do not give me something, I will put out your eyes!" This woman was capable of doing it, or any other kind of crime from hunger, as she had already done many evil acts of violence. So I fetched the grits and divided them with her.

Chapter 11

Conversion In Orenburg And Revival In The Home Village

After my release from the punishment camp I traveled home again. Unfortunately my joy in being home once again was not of long duration, for after only twenty five days I was once again fetched by the police and brought back to forced labor. This time I was sent to the cement block factory part of the brick factory. With eighteen other girls I was housed in one room. Some of them were visiting the Christian congregation in the city of Orenburg, where only Russian was spoken, prayed, and sung. I was invited to come along but could not understand everything, since I had learned only very little Russian as yet. In spite of that I went there gladly, for in me was a longing awakening to also become a child of God. Only I did not know how one could accomplish that.

In my innermost being I wished to be able to see once how someone could get converted. This did not seem possible to me. Never-the-less I prayed, "Lord, I would like to be your child, but I do not know how I should even begin to do that." I would like to have confided my longings to someone, and so I hoped that one of the brethren who did the preaching, would speak to me. But even that did not happen. Then I remembered what my mother had told me. In her village there were two men who were so hardened that perhaps there was no more grace for them. Then I thought to myself, "Am I also one of those who is so hardened?" I had always put off giving my heart to the Lord. Now it was perhaps also too late for me! That oppressed me so much to think of it, that I wanted to cry, but I could not even cry.

As I went to the meeting for the fifth time—that was on the 10th of October, 1948—it seemed to come to me, today is the day of decision!

During the sermon these words fell on my ears: "Today, if you hear his voice, harden not your heart!" Then it seemed to me as though my heart wanted to spring right out of my chest, and I thought: "I don't want to harden my heart. I would like to convert to the Lord. But I don't know how I should even start to do it. Oh, if only someone would help me!"

The meeting came to an end. The people greeted one another and were conversing. But I was so deeply sorrowful, because it seemed to me as though it was too late now for me. Then the young people were invited to come in once more for an after service. I sat down on the last bench. A young preacher by the name of Wena prayed shortly and then gave a testimony of his own life of how he, on New Year's Eve four years ago, had decided for Christ. At that time he was the only young person in the whole congregation. But today there were so many young people. How the angels in heaven must be rejoicing that so many had been converted! I thought: "Yes, the angels will rejoice over the others, but not over me." Then I began to cry bitterly. I bent my head deeply so that no one would be able to see me. But beside me sat Margaret. She noticed what was happening to me and motioned Brother Wena to come over to us. He then asked me why I was so sorrowful in heart. Then I confessed that I wanted to accept the Lord Jesus and he should pray for me. This they then did, and I opened up my heart and invited the Lord Jesus to forgive all my sins and take me as a child of God. After we stood up from our knees, the preacher read to me some words from the Holy Scriptures, and asked me if I now believed that the Lord had forgiven my sins and accepted me as a child of God. Now I could joyfully answer him, "Yes!" Deep happiness and peace flooded my heart. Everyone greeted me and rejoiced with me. From then on I visited the services regularly, and with great joy.

Sometime later I wanted to go home for furlough. I was rejoicing much in the prospect, but at the same time I had reservations, for my brothers and sisters had not yet decided for Christ. Probably I had already written to them of my decision for Christ, and also asked them for forgiveness for all of the unjust things that I had done to them. However, I was still fearful of how I would be accepted. Therefore I prayed daily that God would open the hearts of all my brothers and sisters that they would also clearly decide for him. This prayer request was answered in a wonderful way. A dear acquaintance, Helena Esau, received a letter with the news that a revival had broken out at home and many were being converted. Among them was my sister Katharina.

Shortly after that I received a letter from home and found out that also my sister Helena and my niece, Freda, had also become believers. Now my joy was greater and I could hardly wait anymore until I could get home.

At home a completely new atmosphere prevailed. The people were friendly and helped one another. Evenings they came together and sang songs of faith. They had no preacher, but one or the other would testify of his experience with God, and then several would pray and thank God for his goodness. It was a wonderful time, the time of the first love for the Savior. After fourteen days my furlough was at an end, and I had to go back to forced labor. But now everything was easier to bear for among the girls there were two others of the same conviction, Margareta, and K.T. Their beds stood beside mine, so that we could share with one another and pray together before sleeping. Shortly after that several other girls were converted. I worked with one of the sisters by the name of Justina. We had to shove the heavily loaded carts. My cart was in such bad condition that it was hard to move it from a standing position. Justina often took hold of it and helped me.

The brethren and sisters of the Orenburg congregation covenanted together to pray for one another every evening at eight o'clock, no matter where they would be, whether at home or on the road. That covenant we have faithfully kept to, over the intervening years.

Chapter 12

Temptation And Preservation

In those days we often expressed the wish: "Alas, if only we could just once eat enough bread to be satisfied!" Then came 1949, and it first appeared as if it was a year when this would become possible. Bread ration cards and provision ration cards were abolished, and it was said that now bread could be freely bought and sold. But now new difficulties came up. Already early mornings around 5 o'clock one had to begin to stand in the long lines that were forming. Workers that were just coming back from the night shift had luck many times in buying this bread. But for all those who went to work early in the morning and could not stand in line, it was almost impossible to buy bread. The stores were open around 9 o'clock. At first the people took their places in the long waiting lines in an orderly fashion. But shortly before the opening of the business men came running up screaming and shoving the women away. It came even to riots. Many women were thrown down and became unconscious; it was a miracle that they were not trampled to death.

Once I was thrown into such crowd. The men were pushing and shoving from behind and before and I was lifted up and carried into the air and thought to myself: "If I come out of this experience alive I will never come to get bread again!" I was so shoved and carried right into the store, that I could hardly put my feet on the ground. I hardly got one loaf of bread and all my limbs and breast bone hurt me for a long time afterwards. Within two hours the entire store was sold out. But not nearly all of the people were able to buy bread. It went the same way with other food provisions. You had to stand in line for sometimes four hours. And then when your turn came there was often nothing left to sell. These conditions

78

lasted in this manner for some years until it finally became better.

In the year, 1949, I was still in forced labor. To be sure the food was somewhat better, and yet the work oppressed us as much as always. The production quotas were set too high, and we just could not fill them. The overseers drove us unmercifully. They kept shouting at us: "Girls, faster, faster!" We became completely dispirited. Even though we put all of our energies into the work, it just was not possible to fill the expectant quotas. I became so weak that I would like to have reported myself sick. But I just was not written down as being sick since I did not have a fever. Only those burning with a high fever were permitted to take off work.

Through the winter time we loaded up the dried block in the brick factory of Orenburg. We loaded them on small metal carts, and pushed them to the firing ovens. All along the way we laid down 20 centimeter wide sheet metal. This was so that that carts could roll more easily than over the lumpy, bumpy earth. With rain this ground became sticky and wound itself fast around the wheels. It just could not be avoided. But dirt also got on the sheet metal. As soon as it became wet, it stuck fast to the little iron wheels of the carts so that they would not turn anymore; we could not move them a single step further. For this reason one lady always went ahead and swept away the sticky earth from the pieces of sheet metal. When this earth froze fast, then the wheels skidded and the carts tipped over. If it snowed, it meant more work. Then we had to shovel a way clear through the often three and half foot snow from the factory hall to the bake ovens. Since the lowest level of snow froze fast to the sheet metal, we had to strew salt and then the push carts went faster and tipped over again. Then the command was: "Load up! and forward!" On the long path from the Hall to the bake ovens this happened so often that we were at the point of despair. How could we possibly fill the quota that was set for us? But the bosses had no pity.

One day a mighty temptation presented itself to me. I wanted to make an end of my drudgery because my strength was almost all gone. It seemed impossible to me to hold out any longer. I planned to let my hand be smashed so that I could be then written up as sick and would not have to push the push carts anymore. I went into one of the big sheds where the heavy blocks and bricks were piled up as high as the roof. A long board stood at an angle to the pile and on both sides of the board were other boards used as guides, so that the bricks and blocks that were slid down this board would not fall before they reached the bottom. On top of the pile stood a woman worker who always laid two bricks or blocks on the boards and let them slide down. Down below another woman worker always stood who caught these bricks very carefully and removed them so that one would not be destroyed or broken in two by the one that came next. Then she loaded them on the ready standing carts.

My plan was not to take the one stone away from the sliding board, but to lay my left hand on top of it so that the next stone sliding down would smash my hand. The block rushed down. I trembled as I laid my hand on top of it. Soon the next one roared down. But shortly before striking, it turned itself queerly; my fingers indeed received a hefty blow and the skin was torn, but the hand itself was not smashed. "I'm never going to try that a second time," I thought. Even though I had pain, I kept on working. Now I was healed of my bad idea. When I think back on this today, I cannot understand how this really came about at that time. It was my despair which had driven me to this frightful plan. But the goodness of God had interfered with my plan and protected me from becoming one handed. For that I will always be thankful to him from the bottom of my heart.

Chapter 13

Baptism And Marriage
In Orenburg

After I had made my decision for Christ, I often thought of words in Acts 2:38 — "Repent, and let each of you be baptized in the name of the Lord Jesus Christ for the forgiveness of sins, so you will receive the gift of the Holy Ghost." One day my sister in faith , Maria Schwartz, came to me and asked me, "Don't you want to be baptized?" Surely there is a baptismal feast coming up, and I would like to be baptized myself at that time." "Yes, I would like that, too. We should make it known so tht they can expect us." Whoever wants to belong to one of the registered churches must make a request to the unbelieving officials to decide whether they can allow your baptism or not. We gave our request to the congregational Elder Jakow Jesimowitsch, and he noticed at once that we were still officially too young. I was twenty three, and Maria Schwartz was 24 years old; for under twenty five years of age nobody was permitted to be baptized. After a short time we received the official answer to our request. It was a refusal. This depressed us very much. The lady said to us, "Go anyway by night into the house of the Elder and ask him if he would baptize you anyway. Surely he will not deny you."

So one day I went into the city and as I came into the house of the Elder, my heart was beating hard. I knocked on the door and the elder came out and invited me into his home. Then he asked me what my wish might be, and I told him as well as I could. For a while he considered and then he said, "Good, I will do it. But do not tell anyone else! On the day in which we are going to have a baptismal feast, you appear there, and we will see what can be done." He named for me a forthcoming evening on which I should come before the congregation for examination. With cheerful heart I returned home again. From one girl who had already been baptized I borrowed a baptismal dress. After the examination, I went secretly with some others, on the 29th of August, 1950, to a lake that was deep in a forest, to be baptized. There was no other human being to be seen anywhere except those active in the baptism. As witnesses there were only a few singers standing by. Of the baptismal songs only one verse could be sung softly. Then we went back to the Congregational meeting house where the persons baptized were consecrated by prayer and the laying on of hands. Later on this regulation was somewhat loosened, and the official age limit for baptism was lowered from twenty five to eighteen years.

When the congregation gathered together for worship services, the choir sang (directed by one of the older sisters) beginning with a beautiful hymn. The singers in the choir were composed of at least half of German girls and young men who had been condemned to forced labor. The women wore simple and poor clothing, also very modest hair styling and covering. That pleased the Elders very much; for this did not make so much trouble as with other more well-to-do ladies. The Elders and the other brethren had much compassion on us German ladies and one could feel that from their expressions.

Brother Perepjolkin one day delivered a sermon on verses from I Cor. 7 and I Cor. 13. The main thought of this was that there is a worldly love; and a divine love which is given by God. Each person should put his life in God's hands, and trust him to lead them in the most important question of marriage somewhat like this: "Lord, if you will that I should enter into marriage, then lead me to one who is a like-minded and believing marriage partner. If you do not want this for me, then make me satisfied with your leading and give to me the capacity for living alone for you." Then he told of an experience from the circle of his own acquaintances. A young man learned to know a girl and loved her excessively. It seemed as though there had never been such a great love as this given to anyone. But fourteen days after the wedding this brother passed by the house of the young married couple. Then he heard from inside loud scolding and crying. All at once the house door slammed open, and the young man shoved his young wife out the door, and with a terrible curse spit after her and slammed the door shut. So this is what happened to the "great love"; for it was no love sent from God. I took these words to heart and prayed in this manner: "Lord, if you will that I marry, then arrange everything according to your good will. And if you do not will this for me, then give me as a gift that I should gladly and contentedly accept what you have for me."

And God heard my prayer. He led me and Abram Hamm together. On the 5th of February, 1952, we got our state license for marriage and on the 17th of February, 1952, we celebrated our wedding in the church of the congregation at Orenburg.

1. Maria Braun (center front) in the year 1930 with mother and brothers and sisters.

2. Maria Braun in the year 1950 after her conversion.

3. The parents and brothers and sisters of Abram Hamm in the year 1947-8 (he himself is not on the photo).

4. Abram Hamm in the year 1950 after his conversion.

5. The wedding of Abram and Maria Hamm (maiden name, Braun) on 2-17-1952, in Orenburg.

6. Abram and Maria Hamm, in the year 1953, in Karaguj, with their first son, Heinrich.

Part II

Abram Hamm:
Childhood and Youth

Chapter 1

In The Orenburg Steppes

My homeland lies in the Orenburg district of the southern Ural Mountains. There I, Abram Hamm, was born on the 5th of August, 1930, in the village of Seljonoje. My father, Heinrich Hamm, was a farmer that worked 25 hectares of crop land. After the nationalization of farms, he worked as a carpenter in the collective farm, making wagons, window frames, tools, etc., all out of wood, or repaired the same. My mother, Maria, born Hamm, came from the Ukraine. Both parents were believing Christians. In my birth year, private property was nationalized. Land and agricultural implements were given over to the collective farms. According to the stories my parents told, before the nationalization of land it was at least bearable for them. They could at least feed themselves, and in their life of faith they were left unmolested. Afterwards that was completely different.

To my home village of Seljonoje belonged around 60 families. It was a settlement of those from German background. Their forefathers, in the time of Catherine the Great, came to Russia from low Germany. In the region of Orenburg there were two larger German settlements: The Orenberger Settlement, and the Samara Settlement (also called Luxemburg). My home village belonged to the Orenberger Settlement which included 25 villages. Of those, 22 villages still exist today. Almost all the villages were built along a stream. This was fortunate for economic planning, for then, for example, the livestock could be watered directly from the clear brooks. Seljonoje, however, unfortunately lay far from a stream and this had many consequences. Wells had to be dug and the water pumped out of them. We had to carry the water then to the livestock. Even the people had to fetch water from the wells for their own use.

While I was still a young boy, my parents moved from Seljonoje into the German village of Kamyschow, and from there to another German village Tschornoje-Osero. And again seeking better living conditions, they finally moved to the Russian village of Sapadnoje. There my father had a good income and the Russian Collective Farm boss valued him greatly because he was reliable.

In the summer of 1940 we moved again back to Seljonje. At that time I was 10 years old and it didn't please me at all that we had no stream. This was because I could not learn to swim. When we sometimes went to another village in the summer we saw the boys tumbling about in the stream and swimming. We couldn't do that, and therefore we were mocked and laughed at by them: "You probably bathe yourselves in an ash heap near your house." Beside each house lay an ash heap which had accumulated during the course of the year. We children played around it, and even on top of it but naturally we could not swim in it.

My parents had to work everyday in the collective farm. In the first year they received almost no wages for that. Later it became somewhat better so that families at least could survive from this work.

In the years of the 1930s' there were many bitter times; even famines were common. As children we were often begging Mother — there were seven of us — for something to eat. But besides tears she could give us nothing.

Since there were so many of us as children, my parents gave our sister Susanna to the family of our aunt, the sister of Mother, who also was called Susanna. She and her husband had no children of their own, and wanted to raise Susanna. We often envied Susanna, because she had it so much better than the rest of us. She at least got enough to eat.

My older brothers Heinrich (born in 1919), Jacob (born in 1923), and William (born in 1925) had to help with the work of feeding our large family. They went out into the prairies and trapped the big prairie dogs. These usually weighed from 200 to 600 grams and we could get some meat from them. When my brothers came home from their hunt they skinned the prairie dogs. While I had to help with this, my brothers teased me and held the prairie dogs under my nose. Mother understood how to make a good brew out of these prairie dogs. In its preparation there was an unpleasant smell, but mother knew how to use herbs, salt, onions, and anise to remove the bad flavor. The resulting prairie dog stew tasted exceptionally good to us. "Hunger is the best cook." The best roasts of today still don't taste as good, or give the same satisfaction we experienced in those days from the prairie dog roasts, because of our famine. We boys thought that these prairie dogs were a good catch, even if there was bread. However, when things went better with us economically we let the prairie dogs alone.

The other families also in our village often fed themselves from the prairie dogs. Very few people had any bread or potatoes and therefore had to depend on the prairie dog roasts.

In our district many dogs were running loose that did not belong to anyone. We gave them scraps which they greedily ate. If we could find any that were nourished enough, we caught them and slaughtered them. Many people even slaughtered cats. We didn't do that because the cats were more useful to us to keep down the mice, which would otherwise eat up the rest of our provisions. Even the sparrows were not safe from us boys. We caught them and roasted them in the fire at home, or out in the field. The sparrows had a little bit of good-tasting flesh around the chest.

In spring and summer it was somewhat easier for us boys. Then we would go into the forest and rob the nests of ravens and crows. Their eggs tasted very good to us. We also hunted for sorrell and other edible birds, as well as all kinds of wild berries. If we happened to catch a big prairie dog, then we gathered dried branches and dry grass and made a fire with the matches which we always carried with us and roasted our booty. Edible herbs served as a salad. With them, however, was the danger which we boys were always thinking about that some beautiful looking herbs might not be good to eat. Sometimes someone became sick from them. Even I, once as a six-year-old, had terrible stomach ache because of eating the wrong plants. Fortunately, the poison was mostly eliminated from my system by vomiting. That was my salvation because the only doctor lived four kilometers away from us and could only be fetched by foot and by that time it would be too late for him to come and treat someone who had been poisoned.

In the summer we collected cow manure which lay along side the paths to the meadows, and then we dried it in the sun. This was used for heating; for the woods were too small to provide enough wood.

In 1937, the fields of the collective farm gave a good harvest. Then the collective farm workers were paid with so much wheat that we had to clear out a room in order to store it all. At that time my parents were working on the collective farm and also my oldest 18-year-old brother, and my 17-year-old sister Anna, and my 14-year-old brother Jacob.

The wheat was cooked in water and thinned with a little skim milk, which provided a very good food and something that satisfied. We would have liked to have had flour in order to bake bread, but there were too few mills for grinding it. Only in the village of Kamyschow, a kilometer away from us was there a water mill. Also in the village of Karaguj, four kilometers away, stood a windmill. It naturally could not work unless the wind was blowing. I always had to be on the watch in case it might be moving. This is why I would go up on a hill from time to time, to see if the long wings of the windmill would be moving. As soon as I saw them moving, I ran home and reported the news with great joy. So it happened from time to time that we were able to have ground grain. The flour was used only for the finest things such as noodles.

My parents were rather inventive and made some handmills. They cut some wood pieces to the right size and then put two of these pieces together so that one turned over the other. In between them were set little pieces of metal so that pouring the grain into a hole, on top of the piece turning, allowed it to fall down and be ground up between the two pieces and made finer by the metalic parts. This was rather primitive, but still served to give us a roughly ground grain. The grain was not ground well enough for fine things but just for rough purposes.

In our house we had two rooms of eighteen square meters and a kitchen that was about fifteen square meters in size. The rooms were two and a half meters high. The two double windows could not be opened. They always remained firmly shut and sealed, so that none of the icy winter cold could penetrate. In the winter it was normally below zero and a sharp wind blew constantly. Before winter broke in, most of the houses were surrounded with straw and ashes to further insulate them. For furniture we owned one clothes closet, one table, a pair of stools and a wooden bench on the wall. For sleeping, wooden boards covered with a straw sack served for every two persons. The floor was made of lime and straw and cow dung stamped together. Every spring these floors had to be redone. For this we prepared lime and cow dung outside the house. They were mixed with water into a kind of solution and then plastered into the floors inside from a board. So that the floors in the room would look prettier, the women would decorate them with white chalk. For that they used a glassful of white chalk powder and stamped white rings in different designs on the floor.

Chapter 2

Imprisonment And Testing Of Faith

Since the harvest of 1927 was a plentiful one, we could call this year a golden year. However, at the same time there broke a great wave of persecution over both Christians and non-Christians, insofar as they were no communists. Night after night men were arrested, and disappeared, never to be seen again. I was at the time seven years old and could usually sleep well through the night. But in those terrible, fearful times I would often wake up nights and hear my parents loudly beseeching God. They knelt down, then they stood up, then they went back and forth in the room wringing their hands. Often they looked out of the window in order to see who was being taken away and kidnaped. I could hear the sound of the car motors as they drove by. This caused a cold feeling to go up and down my back and nameless anxiety seized my childish nature. Up to that time I had never seen a car; for in the collective farm there were only small tractors. Only ten years later did they receive a one and a half ton pickup truck. We called the feared police-cars in Russian "Tschjornyj woron," That means "Black Ravens". They were painted black and came in the night. At that time also the miller, Franz Löwen, was arrested and taken away. His windmill had started to go round and round during a big storm, and the friction caused it to burn down. He was accused of not doing all that he could to save his windmill, and so he was condemned as a saboteur. Franz Löwen never did come back and his wife had to see to it to raise their three sons, Heinrich, Jacob, and Peter, by herself.

After such nights in which men were arrested, great excitement reigned in our village, and bitter sorrow stuck with those of the relatives who were left behind. Even my Uncle Abram Hamm, who had up to this time

worked as a brigadier in the collective farm in Seljonoje, was arrested and
never came back. His wife Susanna, and son Willie, and daughter Lena
remained behind in poverty. I was able to baptize them later in the year,
1957, and take them into our congregation of believers.

In the year, 1937, my father took a special education course, as an ac-
countant, in the village of Kamenka, which was thirty kilometers away in
the village of Alexandrofski. From all the villages of the district men were
sought to volunteer to study to be accountants. The communist officials
used this also to try to exterminate the Christian faith. One day some commissars came to the school and demanded that all of the participants sign
themselves on a list as atheists. They went from one to the other and each
one had to sign. Some of them were Christians. They thought perhaps that
they could remain Christian in heart, because God looks on the heart (I
Sam 16:70). Many-a-one must have trembled to do this because of the
inner struggle but still out of fear, most of them signed. My father sat in
the second to the last row and sighed deep in his heart to the Lord. One of
the Commissars came to him and demanded that he also sign himself up
with this list. But my father answered, "I can never do that! I am a Christian!" Every one turned around to stare at him, and everyone wondered
what would happen next. One of the commissars screamed, "What? You
are a Christian? Such a thing does not exist anymore?" My father answered, "Never-the-less! Never-the-less! I cannot sign and I will not do
it!" He knew exactly that by this kind of a stand, he was putting his profession, his family, and his freedom in danger. Now they came to his neighbor in that row who also did not sign, but would rather go to prison than to
deny his Lord Jesus Christ. Because of this, my father was accused of being an agitator. The neighbor, however, declared at once that he had not
been influenced by him but had taken this stand out of his own free will.

After that, my father asked other Christians who had signed themselves
as atheists, how they could square their signature with their faith. They
justified themselves saying, "We have not denied the Lord in our hearts. In
spite of the signature we still believe in the Lord Jesus Christ." But my
father reminded them of the words of Jesus in Matthew 10:33; Whoever
denies me before men, him will I also deny.

From that point on my parents waited night after night for the Black
Raven to pay us a visit also. My sister Elizabeth and I slept with our parents in one room. For that reason we experienced much fear everytime a
car drove through the street and our parents cried out to the Lord for help.
My mother noticed that I lay weakly in bed and stared at her with anxious

eyes. So she said to me in our Platt-Deutsch or Low German dialect, "Go to sleep Abram." Then I pulled the covers over my head and tried to sleep.

We could only ascribe it to God's protecting grace and providence that my father was not arrested and taken away. He was permitted to remain with his family, and October, 1951, he went home in peace to God. In the cemetery of Karaguj he lies buried. The others however, who had signed themselves as atheists, gradually fell away from the faith little by little, yet they were still arrested. No man knows to this day where they were taken.

7. Abram Hamm's family, 1964, standing in front of their house in Iwanowka which is used by the congregation to this day as a place for worship.

Chapter 3

Dashed Hopes For Emigrating

Almost two hundred years before the Empress Kathrine the Great had invited Germans to emigrate to Russia, they settled in the Ukraine, on the Volga, in the Crimean Peninsula, in the Caucasus, later in the Orenberger District, in the southern Ural Mountains, and also in Siberia and Middle Asia. During the second World War all of those in the Ukraine, in the Volga District, and in the Crimea were shipped to Siberia, or in the far North, or far East. Those Germans living in Orenberg, and Middle Asia and in Siberia, had women, men and youth drafted for forced labor with very few exceptions. Later when the resident's restrictions were lifted, Germans settled according to their own desires in many other districts of Russia, so that today almost everywhere in the wide Soviet Union Germans can be found.

In the year, 1940, Germans living in Seljonoja and in other districts were excited by the great hope to emigrate back to Germany. Time and again they spoke about it and pictured how it would be if they could return to their homeland out of which their forefathers had come. We children listened to such conversations attentively and could not hear enough of them. My mother toasted Zweiback bread and hung it in a bag in the loft. This was supposed to be our travel provision. At that time I was in the third grade in school and from great excitement at the forthcoming emigration I gave away all my school books to Russian school boys. Two Russian families lived in our village. Later when our hopes of emigration were dashed, I was sorry that I had done this.

Even my parents waited longingly for the day when the journey would come, although already once in the year, 1929, they had been bitterly disillusioned at prospects of emigration. At that time they wanted to travel out to the West to western Europe and had already sold or given away all their things. With their five children they came to Moscow where already many families were squatting in railroad stations and private quarters. While they waited to emigrate, the two year old daughter, Maria, became ill and died. That was a terribly painful loss. Furthermore, my parents had the complications of running from one office to the other until they finally got permission to bury the child in a cemetery. Then came the hardest blow of all for them. It was made known that nobody was allowed to leave the country. Everybody must go back to their home villages. So my parents returned 1300 kilometers to the Orenberger district. Their they had to find out how to survive with their four living children. Since they no longer had their possessions, having sold or given away everything, the prospect was gloomy. However, many people returned what had been given to them. But the few things that they got back of their agriculture implements, cattle and land were once again taken away from them in the general confiscation of the year, 1930, and given over to the collective farm.

Despite these bitter experiences, in the year, 1940, my parents' hearts were once again overcome with the hope to finally be able to emigrate out of the Soviet Union, the land in which they had experienced so many difficulties. But even this hope had to be buried when Hitler invaded Russia with his war. How we Germans were then condemned as "Fritzes," "Faschists," and "Hitlerpack!" But it was not our fault that Hitler, who himself was not even a German, but an Austrian, wanted to conquer the whole world. We would have much preferred it if there had been no war at all, with its many injustices, much bloodshed, and many tears.

In March of 1942, German men from 16 years old and up with few exceptions were drafted for forced labor. Most women whose children were three years old or older were also taken into forced labor. Many children had to stay back without parents and were divided up among relatives. My parents were not drafted to forced labor; this was because my father was an invalid, and could only go very slowly. He had been run down once when he was thirty years old, in an accident in the snow. At this time one of his legs was dislocated from his hip. My mother at this time was already fifty three years old. Since work had to go on in the collective farm, my parents and their children were taken up for this.

Chapter 4

Many Dangers And Providences

Once when I was twelve years old I had to go nights with Cornelius Litke, the same age as myself, to herd horses on the plains. We would have much rather stayed in bed than to be out in the dark night alone on the prairies. It was so dark, that one could not see his hand before his eyes. As a leaden tiredness crept over us, we sought for a straw or haystack, made a hole in it and laid down. We had terrible fear of the wolves even though they seldom attacked people in summer because then they could find enough other victims. However, in winter they often attacked people. We did not dare to let the horses run loose because they could have gotten lost. So that this would not occur, we tied the horses with a ten meter long rope. One end was tied to our foot. So they had enough free room to be eating. But there was one danger with that, that we had not even considered. Our parents made us aware of it later: namely that the wolves could have frightened the horses, and they could have raced away dragging us children along behind them. My mother said, "Surely a guardian angel protected you."

In July, 1942, I had once laid down in the shade beside our house. I fell asleep and did not even notice how the sun shone and came around the corner and shone strongly on my head. When I woke up I felt very sick and towards evening I was seriously ill. The night was bad. The next morning my father hitched up the horse and took me to the doctor. He said, "You have had a sunstroke!" He gave me a mild, white liquid to drink and ordered that I would stay inside the house for three days. Only if the sun was behind the clouds would I be allowed to go out.

In December, 1942, some boys and I hitched up a horse to the sled and chased over the wide prairie flats with it. We drove the horse at the fastest speed. I sat backwards in the sled directly behind the horse. All at once the horse kicked back and struck me on the back of my head. I fell from the sled while my comrades drove on laughing out loud. I pulled myself up, my hat was gone, my head pained terribly, and crying I went home. The place on my head where I was struck swelled and made a lump as big as a hen's egg. Slowly it healed, but after a few months it swelled up again, broke open and some bone splinters came out.

In the summer of 1945, food of any kind was scarce. I went into the wheat fields of the collective farm nearby, in order to see if I could get some ripe wheat. Actually, I soon found some ripe heads. Since I had such great hunger, I rubbed the wheat kernels open and for once ate enough to feel really satisfied. Then I went home. There I felt a great thirst and drank a lot of water. But this did not react well because my body began to swell and hurt me terrible. I hardly knew what to do with myself because of the pain. Still with the help of God I came through this danger, too.

To be sure I was not drafted into forced labor like the other Germans because I was still too young. And now the war was at an end. But I was supposed to go in place of a young Russian by the name of Kriwopalow in the FSO (Labor Service). I fought against this and rather wanted to run away. It was in July of 1946, shortly before the harvest. Since we had no more bread, my mother gathered beet leaves from the field and cooked out of it a soup, also putting in a few potatoes and eggs.

I had mind to travel to my brother Willie who lived 100 kilometers away in the village of Kutorle, which was in German Samara. First I had to go about 30 kilometers through the German settlement, then through a settlement of Russians, Baschkiren and Morwinen. On the journey I would have to beg my bread, but unfortunately could not find any. I could speak Russian well, so that nobody would notice that I was German. Once I came to a house out of which an old lady and her daughter were coming. I greeted them in a friendly manner, bowed, and begged for a piece of bread. Then said the old lady in German, "We ourselves have nothing." Because I had spoken in Russian, the daughter translated for me, what their mother had said, into Russian. I had to go on my way hungrily. I was not really sure of the way, and I did not have a map. From village to village I kept asking. And so I came to the village of Kutorle on the evening of the second day. The last 3 kilometers to my brother Willie's house I walked with some ladies who had been out on the prairies milking their cows. He still had some bread and even some potatoes, but I did not imagine that I could stay long with him, because it was still too near to my own village, and the police could have been able to find me very easily. Therefore, I planned to go to my cousins, Willie and Johann Dıumuckmann, who had been resettled in a place called Korkino in the Tscheljabinsk District.

My brother Willie gave me 50 Rubels, a loaf of bread and some vegetables; he could not do more for me. This money I would have used for food, but not for a ticket. So like many others I tried to travel on the black market. That means to go up on the roof of the train cars. We call this in Russian "Sajtschikom." That means like a rabbit or like a secret passenger. So I left from Sorotschinsk on the 4th of August. All the train car roofs were fully occupied. Some young men had even put their bicycles up there. At every stop of the train we were chased down by the police. But as soon as the train was in motion once again, we hung on, crept up and jumped from wagon to wagon until each one had his own place once again. To travel to Tscheljabinsk—Korkino I had at least two days and two nights ahead of me. During the day it was durable, because it was in summer, even though the wind of traveling whistled past our ears. But nights it was so cool, and we had to creep down into the ends of the train cars. I was so tired that I could hardly hold myself upright anymore. For this reason I lay down on the roof and fastened both hands around the chimney in order not to fall off (in Russian trains there are usually ovens to heat tea and for cooking). Before falling asleep I thought to myself, "This is my birthday!" It was the fifth of August. That I was not thrown off of the roof while I was asleep, I attribute only to the providence and grace of God.

Early in the morning (it was still very cool) a young fellow came up on the roof and said, "I'm freezing!" "Give me your jacket!" When I refused, he wanted to throw me off the roof. What was left for me to do, but to take off my jacket and give it to him? Then he demanded my money. However, I had this hidden in my socks, and showed him only my empty purse. In it was nothing except a small knife that my brother Willie had given me as a present. The man took it away from me. I begged him, "Give me at least your jacket so that I won't freeze!" He left me his thin jacket and did not take my bread from me. That was one of the good bandits. Some hours later another one came and demanded my bread. When I refused he stuck two fingers of his right hand out and said, "Give it here or I'll pick out your eyes!" I gave him the bread and begged him at the same time to give me just a little piece of it back. Matter-of-factly he gave me a piece back.

When I came to my cousins I found that they had nothing for me to eat. So then I went into the forest and hunted for berries which I could sell at the market place. In this way I could buy some bread and some oat grits. We cooked them with water and ate them together. Then I went looking for work but nobody would take me on because I had no official papers with me. There were too many tramps and runaways and I was held to be such a person. So one month went by and I said to myself like the lost son in the parable of Jesus, "I will get up and go home to my parents. Now it is autumn and my parents will have gotten bread from the collective farm, and in the garden we can find potatoes, beets, etc." Going back home again I also traveled "black market."

At one stop when we were all chased down from the roofs it happened to me that I wasn't quick enough when the train started up again and I was left behind. The next train had several empty cars in which cement and coal were being transported. I crept into a coal car and rejoiced that I was able to be there all alone. It was dark and from the open car I could see out at the stars as I traveled. At one station all the cars were searched and then I was discovered. A rough voice said, "Get out! Otherwise I will beat you like a dog!" I was glad that I could disappear and not be arrested.

As it became morning again another passenger train came again in the direction of Orenberg. I saw how two boys had crawled under one car in a reserve chest kept for the coal and a third from outside had made closed the cover and went away. I crept along the car until I found an empty chest for myself, looking all around and then crept into the chest and shut it. I held myself as still as a mouse until in about two minutes the train left. Through the cracks I could see the gleaming railroad tracks under me. It was probably an express train for it did not stop often. At each stopping place I had fears that I would be discovered and arrested. But finally we came to Orenburg. I crept out of my dogs chest and found out that my hands were black from coal dust. I couldn't see my face but I noticed that people were staring at me strangely. I asked another boy, "Why are the people looking at me like that, how do I look?" he said, "Like a nigger!" So then I looked for water and washed myself. Then I met two young men who were also going in the direction of my home. We decided how we would best proceed. Just at that moment police came and arrested us and put us into jail. Probably they were looking for a certain criminal because after four hours we were released again. With the next train I traveled to Pokrowka, from where I still had to walk 45 kilometers on foot. Fortunately a horse and wagon passing by, took me along. So after about two month's absence I came home again to my parents. It seemed to me as if I had been gone for ten years. How my parents house seemed so good to me!

On the 18th of September, 1947, — meanwhile I had turned 17-we were threshing the wheat harvest with a horse-drawn threshing machine. I fetched the wheat with a horse and wagon, loaded it up in the threshing machine, and then helped my friend Peter Löwen. He stood in the middle of the platform and drove the horses which were hitched by four pairs, one behind another, and going around in a circle. He drove them with a long whip. All at once this whip broke and the broken part fell beside the gears. Without thinking I bent over to pick up the broken piece of whip. And while I was looking at the beam on which the horses were pulling, so that it would not hit me, I groped with my right hand down below and stuck it into the gear! The horses did not stop and there was only a small jerk and three of my fingers were torn off! If I had gone lower or further into the gears it would have taken off my entire arm. I stood up and grabbed my wounded hand with my left hand and ran away from the place and sat on a stone. There I sat until Peter and several other young men came along. "You're as white as chalk," they said. Then they hitched a horse onto a little wagon and drove me into a neighboring village to the doctor. He only laid some cotton on it and bound my hand with a bandage. Then I was taken back again.

With the little pick-up truck of the collective farm they brought me 45 kilometer's distance to the hospital in Pokrowka. My comrades had loaded the truck full of straw on which I lay. My father sat beside me and said, "Abram, forget not to pray!" In the hospital we found that the surgeon was not there. So once again cotton was laid on my wound and it was bound up anew but the blood soaked through. Not until the third day did the surgeon from Orenburg come back. It was a lady doctor. She at once ordered an operation. When I awoke from the drug, I was lying in bed. Only after 45 days was I allowed to come home. It was a miracle that no blood poisoning set in, for the wound was full of dirt for three long days.

Chapter 5

Revival And Persecution In The Orenberg District

Since the years of the 30's, the congregation and believers seemed to be dead; and to the authorities it appeared as though there were hardly any Christians anymore. But during the war God graciously gave a revival to those who lived in the Ukraine; where many people, and young people as well, were converted to a living faith in Jesus Christ as Lord! Even in the Samara Settlement, which before the war consisted of fourteen villages (today there are only 12), hundreds of people decided for Christ during the revival time. The Christians who had lost their courage woke up, confessed their sins and let themselves be purified by the blood of Jesus. So there arose new life in every village. The believers gathered themselves together in private houses. Simple men preached because there were no preachers anymore.

But also the accuser of the brethren did not rest. He stirred up the communist authorities. It just didn't suit them that Christian living would rise again; especially since they had thought that they were finally finished with that. Now they grabbed sharply at the believers and in September of 1951, arrested 8 persons from the Samara settlement: Johann Peter, Peter Penner, Kornelius Dück, Gerhard Dürksen, J. Janzen, Sister Gersez, Willi Sawatzke and Brother Voth. The first six were condemned to 25 years in concentration camp and the last two because of their advanced age were condemned to 10 years. But they showed themselves as true witnesses of Jesus even in the camps, and through their testimony many prisoners came to a living faith. In the villages the Lord awakened new men, who took the place of the arrested ones in the service of the Gospel. Also in other districts and regions Christians were seized and shipped away to the icy regions of the north. There, through living testimony, new congregations also arose.

In March of 1952, the believers in the city of Orsk in the Orenberg District experienced hard persecutions. Nine men were arrested: Hermann Reimer, Alexander Giesbrecht, Peter Warkentin, (today in Detmold), H. Schmidt, D. Redekop, P. Lehn, J. Basvetter, K. Gross and G. Japz. They were condemned to 25 years in concentration camp with 5 years of exile to follow. Brother Redekop as the youngest received 25 years of concentration camp and 3 years of exile.

Since the autumn of 1947, a revival had also begun in our Orenberger Settlement. It lasted for several years. In the villages the word was: "When no preacher is there, let anyone who can preach." So simple men stood up and exposited the Word of God. The believers came together in private houses, because there simply were no more meeting houses there. Then a new storm broke loose. In the autumn of 1952, there were 18 brothers and 2 sisters out of our settlement arrested: Daniel Peters, Kornelius Giesbrecht (from village 1), Gerhard Rempel (from village 3), Jacob Pankratz — now in Espelkamp —, Peter Esau, Paul Peters, Johann Neufeld, David Enns (from village 4), Johann Unruh (from village 6), Wilhelm Block (from village 7), Johann Neudorf, Johann Töws, Peter Wiebe — now in Gummersbach — , Sister Warkentin (from village 8), Johann Hubert, Sister Peters (from village 10), Heinrich Unruh (from village Kubanka), Peter Siemens (from village Platowka), Dietrich Rempel (from village Stephanowo), H. Heinrichs (from the village of Alisowa). The investigation before the trial drew out to three and a half months. And the trial itself took place from the 15th to the 25th of January of 1953, in Orenberg. All twenty believers received 25 years in concentration camps — that's 500 years in prison altogether — , because they had dared to preach the Gospel in Stalin's time. After Stalin's death in 1953, those of the prisoners who were still alive, including those from Orsk and out of our Orenberger settlement, were gradually rehabilitated and let go into freedom. So God worked in those days.

Chapter 6

God's Grace Reached Even Me

I myself was raised by believing parents. My father owned a New Testament which was already old and torn. Yet my parents held it in honor, and always read from it every evening. They had taught me also a children's prayer: "Dear Savior, Make me pious, so that I might come into heaven." At the table my father always spoke a prayer, and with it we stood up. When my father was not there then Mother prayed. As I became older I became conscious that memorized exercises could not satisfy God, but I myself would have to make a decision, and become converted.

Later in the autumn of 1947, a revival began in our village; also, many were converted. People of all denominations-Lutherans, Baptists, Mennonites, and members of the Brethren-came together to sing, to pray and to praise God. At that time no one asked to which group a person belonged; only later did it come to disagreements because of different conceptions and teachings. Also my sister Anna was converted at that time and she was so happy through that experience. I would have done it, too, but I didn't know how I should even begin. I asked my mother, and she said, "Pray about it, and the Lord will grant it to you." I thought that something special had to happen from the outside, or that one had to do something himself.

On the 19th of February, 1948, I heard that a girl of my age wanted to become converted. At the evening worship service I sat down on a bench behind this girl and wanted to observe how that could happen, because I wanted to do the same thing myself. But I waited in vain for her conversion. Up to that time I had always thought: "I am however a decent person", because I didn't smoke, I didn't curse, and I kept myself from many unjust things. Now, however, I recognized with fright that I was a lost sinner, lost for eternity. Then a struggle began in me. What should I do that I might be saved? My friends Abram Peters and David Dück, who sat to the right and to the left of me, could not have noticed anything of my condition. Until slowly tears began to run down my cheeks. Then everyone stood up to pray. Now I couldn't hold back anymore, and I broke out into weeping and fell back on the bench. I cried out loud, "Lord, forgive me my sins!" God saw that I was in earnest. He gave me the complete assurance that my sins were forgiven for Jesus' sake. I could believe it and a deep joy filled my heart. Then I thanked my God out loud for it. The congregation sang the song: "Is it true that Jesus died for me and atoned for my guilt? That the Lamb of God suffered for me on the cross. Oh wonderful mercy! On the Cross, On the Cross, light dawned in my heart, and my blind eyes were opened, for I let the Savior into my heart. Hosanna, now is peace from God my experience."

Also my friend Abram Peters was converted the same evening. However, the girl whom I had sat behind to see how one could get converted, did not yet find that experience. To this day I rejoice over it that I did not have to watch another's experience, but that Jesus himself worked that work in me.

After the worship service I hurried home and told my experience to my father who lay sick in bed. How he rejoiced in his heart! He stood up and prayed with me. Then he gave me practical counsel how I could continue to be obedient to the Spirit of God. "Make good the past injustice and sins, and live daily with the Lord," said he. I begged my father, "Please write down for me a prayer." My father answered, "Good, I will write a short prayer for you. However if you are truly born again you will not need that for very long, because you will be able to pray from your own heart."

In the next worship service many prayed one after another. I wanted to pray, too, but as soon as one prayer was over, another started to pray. Sweat broke out on my forehead. But finally there was a pause in the series. I spoke up loudly and quoted the prayer that I had learned from my father and a few more words that I added to it. That was the first and also the last time that I had to pray with a memorized prayer.

From this time on I was a Christian. I am thankful that that Lord found me. He alone gave my life meaning, not my own works or my own decency. Through His grace I am what I am. And He will lead me my whole life long and at last to my blessed goal.

Before my conversion I had often secretly thought about a girl without ever having mentioned anything about it to anyone. But after my conversion this feeling was gone, without anything done on my own part, as though it were extinguished. So much did my new life in God fill me. He also did want to make clear to me that he did not approve of this girl that I had been thinking about for my future wife.

Chapter 7

Denial And Secret Meetings

In the face of this revival, naturally, also, the accuser of the brethren began his work again. The communists forbade the gatherings and threatened us with arrests. Mindful of the years of the 1930's when so many had been brought into concentration camps, many were frightened, especially of the older Brothers and Sisters and ceased having worship services. The other Brethren and Sisters, especially the younger ones, never-the-less kept coming together, to read God's Word, pray, and sing.

I had begun to feel responsible for the youth, and led out in our meetings. We were very cautious about how we conducted this, but in spite of that, the officials heard of it. I was summoned and threatened with prison. Then I became frightened, and signed that I would from now on hold no more youth meetings in my house, also that I would attend no more. I tried to calm my conscience with this thought, "I have not really denied God himself!" But of this occurrence I told no one.

On the next Sunday evening I crept behind the houses until I reached that house where the youth had gathered themselves. Since the houses had thick outer walls the entrance was always constructed of double doors. Like a thief I crept softly between the two doors and listened to what they were saying inside. One of them asked the others, "But where is Abram? Is he sick?" Others answered, "No, we saw him today at work." (Until late in the autumn we had no days of rest, even on Sundays we had to work). Nobody knew what was wrong; I had not told anyone. So it went for two long Sundays. As soon as the congregation was getting ready to dismiss, then I crept softly away.

My conduct left me no rest, until I finally spoke to my father about it.

To be sure he wanted to hear nothing about my going into prison, but even less that I should be untrue to the Lord. It became clear to me that whatever comes out of this I will go again into youth work. That's the only way for me to be joyful again. If I think back on that today, I am surprised and ashamed of myself, that I could ever sign anything like that. God had forgiven me my denial. I had to learn that I, without his help, was only a nothing. And I can understand those, too, who likewise today deny. I can't lift myself up over them and remain, as it were, proud and self-righteous about their conduct. Without the power of Jesus I would be ready for every denial and capable of every betrayal. Of that I am convinced.

Even though the war was at an end, we had in the years from 1949 to 1951, to go through very difficult times. To be sure we were not really actually starving anymore, but meals were scanty. Also we possessed very little clothing. If something was washed or needed to be mended, then we had nothing else to put on, and had to remain in bed. In the wartime and also for a long time after the war we had a great plague of insects; fleas, lice, and bedbugs tortured us everywhere. Each evening we had to give up all of our clothing, and while we laid in bed Mother sat until midnight or longer and searched out the lice and fleas in our clothing. She always had a very red thumbnail covered with the blood of these pests. She tried hot ironing, to overcome these plagues. But they multiplied so quickly, that the next morning there were just as many again. Only in the years of the '50s did we receive a white insect powder and life became easier.

In the winter of 1949, I learned that in the village of Pokrowka my job would be gardener; and I followed this work for two years in the collective farm.

The worship services were still forbidden, to be sure, but we could not live anymore without fellowship around the Word of God. And so we sought other ways, in which we could come together to worship Him. Since all the villagers worked on the collective farm, everyone knew each other quite intimately. So we also knew in which house the believing Christians lived. Evenings we went past the houses and if we saw a place where there were no curtains in front of the windows or no dog tied outside we could unnoticed walk up to the window to see who was inside and who had visitors. There we could make ourselves at home; and by signs such as hanging a cloth in the window, go inside so that nobody could notice what we were doing. There we read God's word, prayed and sang our hymns softly. In the daytime during work we gave testimony of our belief and many listened to it. For a time, we youthful ones went to the houses where old believers lived, sang there for them and then ran quickly away to another house. Many of them were asleep already when we sang. They woke up and thought perhaps it was a heavenly visitation that they heard. One lady, for example, woke up, quickly awakened her man and said, "Listen! The angels are singing! Perhaps soon we will hear the trumpet of God and the Lord will come and will fetch his own away!"

During the persecution time we also used the occasion of birthdays as an excuse to come together. Birthday children received a small present, and then we held our worship service. If officials happened to come by to drive us away from one another, then we said, "It is not forbidden to cele-brate a birthday." Then they left us alone, but sometimes they investigated afterwards to see if it were true. On such occasions we thought of the scripture "Be wise as serpents and harmless as doves." What we said in answer was always the truth, measured with the scripture "Let your com-munication be 'Yea, yea; Nay, nay: for whatsoever is more than these cometh of evil.' " Matt. 5:37.

Chapter 8

Engagement And Marriage

God's Word says, "It is not good for man to be alone, I will make a help meet for him." Gen. 2:18

We traveled from time to time to Orenburg, in order to get wood, coal, cattle feed, and replacement parts for our autos and tractors for the collective farm, or to sell our wares from Kolchose. At such times we visited the registered Baptist Church of Orenberg, and got to know believing young people. My brother Jacob found his wife Margarite (born Siemens) there.

My future wife Maria, born Braun, was taken away to forced labor in the region of Orenburg, along with many other girls. She attended the worship services of the Baptist Church in Orenburg, and so I learned to know Maria. Soon it was clear to me that she should become my wife. One day I asked her if she would become my wife; for it was clear to me that we belonged together. She answered, "I don't know about that! I must first have clarity from the Lord before I can say 'yes.' That is a decision for all my life, and I have to pray about it." "We could at least write one another letters," I said. "No, that I will not do! I have so many brothers and sisters to whom I must write, and my mother; I also have to write to her. So I cannot write to you! I don't want to be made a point of conversation by other people!" I wrote to her anyway several times and asked her always the same question: "Do you now at last have clarity?" Only once did I receive an answer, "I still have no clarity!" Two long years did I have to wait.

Several times I thought, "Surely in our village there are other believing young girls. Why should I wait on Maria? Anyway she is three years older than I am." I prayed, "Lord, show me which one of the girls of our village

I should marry!" But I got no assurance that I should choose any of the girls from our village.

One day I traveled again from the collective farm to Orenburg and met Maria. We conversed together, and prayed also together, but I said nothing, not a word of my thoughts and I took leave of her. Later she told me, "Just on that day I was ready to give you my word, Yes! But you did not even ask me. I thought, Now it's over, and he is not even interested in me anymore."

Some months later I had to go again to Orenburg. "Today I will ask her, and may it go as it will!" It was wholly wonderful! Hardly had I asked when she said to me, "Yes, it is now clear to me that we belong together. One thing however I have to tell you. Even though I have the conviction that the Lord has drawn us together, I'm not sure that I really love you!" I breathed a sigh of relief, that now the decision was finally made, and I replied to her, "If the Lord has drawn us together, then he will also give you love for me!"

Three months later in January of 1952, I visited Maria again. Matter-of-fact, the Lord had in between given her a love for me. We spoke about when we would celebrate our marriage. Maria thought, "That cannot be arranged so quickly!" But I immediately said, "But soon you will get vacation and then not another one until another year later! Should we still wait a whole year?" My father had taught me it is not good to wait for a long time to be married once you have chosen one another. When two are engaged, they should soon marry. This I told to Maria and she also saw that it was reasonable, and so we agreed together to wait no longer. She said, "Good, then we will announce our engagement, and marry on my next vacation. As soon as my vacation time is known, I will send you a telegram when I am coming home." With that I was satisfied and took leave of her happily.

Two weeks later I received a telegram. Then my sister Anna drove me with a horse and sled to the village where Maria's mother lived. There we celebrated our engagement with about 200 guests. There wasn't really much food there as we all had so little. A few days later we traveled to Karaguj where my mother and my sisters, Elisa and Anna, prepared a little engagement party for us with about 60 persons. On the 5th of February, 1952, we were officially written down together as married persons. After that we visited our relatives to introduce ourselves as a young married pair, and on the 17th of February, 1952, we were married in the registered Baptist Church by a Russian brother. At the wedding itself we had only 70 guests because we did not have enough provisions to invite any more. In better times weddings often had as many as 500 invited guests. We received as gifts many things for our housekeeping. After three days I traveled back to my village to resign from my work in the collective farm in order to go to Orenburg, and to Maria. But the collective farm would not give me leave because they were short of workers! Now we were married but could not live together. A month later a collective farm meeting was announced and my request was denied again. First Maria had said "No" to me for two long years and now it was the collective farm meeting. What should I do? There stood two old men in the collective farm meeting and they began to speak: "We were all young once and got married. Why should we try to tear apart this young marriage?" So suddenly they all decided to release me.

At the end of March I traveled to Orenburg to my wife. She still had no separate dwelling. She lived with twelve girls together in one room. But two weeks later we finally succeeded in getting a "dwelling." It was only twelve square meters big. It was only a room and under the entrance-way floorboards, there was a tiny cellar, a hole about one meter square in which one could put potatoes for the winter. The toilet was outside. We possessed no table and no chairs. My wife had prepared a bed that was welded together out of iron pieces. All the rest of our worldly goods we had in two suitcases, that was all.

We bought ourselves an alarm clock, because my wife still had to work in a changing shift. Sometimes from 8:00 in the morning to 4:00 in the afternoon, then from 4:00 in the afternoon till midnight, and occasionally from midnight to 8:00 in the morning.

The second thing we bought was an oil stove with which we could cook, for the little hearth which we used for heating in winter, meanwhile we could use to sit on.

From my father, who had gone home to heaven a year before, I inherited some tools. Up to this time I had never made any furniture; only now and again had I watched my father at his work. But now was the time for me to begin to make our own furniture. I begged or bought wood and nails, and then went to work. At first I made a sitting bench and a rocking chair. I had to put everything together on the floor, kneeling because I had no work bench. Soon my knees hurt me very much. Next I made a table with a drawer, then a little bit of a cupboard, a chest and a clothes press which was one meter wide, about fifty centimeters deep and 1.8 meters high. now we had so much furniture that we could hardly move around in our room. After a year as we awaited our first child, I made a crib, which was also put into our dwelling. In this time I began work as a carpenter in an Orenburg brick factory.

Part III

Abram and Maria Hamm:
Life Together

Part III

Chapter 1

Moving To Karaguj

Maria: On February 14, 1953, our first child was born. We rejoiced very much and were proud that it was a son. We named him Heinrich after his grandfather. For one month before and after the birth I did not need to go to work. Then I applied for leave and could remain at home with the child until the 15th of April. In spite of my marriage and the birth of our child I was still held fast in the forced labor sentence.

One day my husband said, "Maria, Why don't we move to my village of Karaguj?" "How could I ever get permission for that?" I asked. "I have asked the officials more than a few times to release me so that I could go and nurse my old mother. I have certificates from the collective farm and from the doctor which I produced to prove that my mother needs my help, but all my applications have been denied. They just will not release me! We cannot find any good reasons to move to Karaguj. Besides what would we want to do there. There I know no one, and there is no congregation there. It is much better here. At least here we have our livelihood."

But my husband answered, "Maria, I have the inner assurance that we should move to Karaguj. Let's ask the Lord to help us. Perhaps He will work it out. Let's try it once and present a proposition to the authorities. We will write them that we are married and would like to move to my old mother's home in the village of Karaguj. If they permit it, then it is the will of God." "Well we can try it, but they are never going to release me," I said. We prepared our proposition and I brought it to the commander of the camp in Orenburg. He replied that in one month I would have their decision.

After this period of time elapsed—it was the 8th of October—I went again to the commander. He pulled out a paper and said, "Your application is permitted. You can move to Karaguj. Report yourself to the authorities there on the 16th of October." In the first moment my understanding could not comprehend it, for I had reckoned on another rejection. He noticed that and said, "It is true! Go and report yourself there!"

At home my husband immediately asked, "Well, what do you have for news?" I laughed and said, "The permission." — "You're probably just joking," he said. "No! Really, It is so!" "I can hardly believe it!" Then I showed him the permit. Now he was astonished, too. Then he said, "So, let's travel at once. It is God's will. He wants to use us in that place."

Now we did not hesitate any longer. On the 15th of October, 1953, we loaded our belonging together into a truck which the Karaguj collective placed at our disposal, and we traveled there. My mother-in-law lived with a married daughter and her son in two rooms, only 35 square meters in size altogether. Now we three were moving into that small space in addition. It was very crowded but we were all happy that it was obvious we had been led there. On the next day I reported myself to the local authorities; and this I had to do each month in order to report that I was present. Only in March of 1956, was regulation lifted and one could live where one wanted to.

Chapter 2

Church Growth In Karaguj

Abram: In Karaguj we soon made connections with other believers and came together in private houses, first in little groups. We sang, prayed and read together God's Word. But we had nobody who could exposit God's Word for us. Furthermore, there was still the anxiety in many hearts that came from the trial hardly a year before in which Brethren and Sisters from our Orenberger Settlement had been condemned to twenty five years in prison.

Many months the thought never left me that I could be used in the service of the Gospel. But I could hardly read German, being fluent only in reading directions. Bibles were all too scarce in the congregation. Mostly we had only hand written songs and poems in Russian and German. Whoever owned a Bible, was regarded to be very rich. We were among these rich ones for each of us possessed a half Bible. We soon understood that the Lord had led us to this village, not only because of my mother, but because he had wanted to put me in the service of the Gospel.

One evening in the year 1954, we were gathered together at Franz Löwen's house. Then I was pressed in the spirit by God to stand up and say something on the words of Psalm 23:1-6. Sweat broke out of all my pores, but I fought through the struggle and was at peace. Let come what may, I would accept it calmly from God's hand.

After this meeting I told my wife about it, who because of our little son's sickness had to stay at home. (Six months after our move he died.) Her first words were, "They will stick you in jail!" How could I think anything else myself, for we had always had persecutions, arrests and trials! For my own part I would have gladly given up preaching, if the Lord had not given me courage and strength for it. I was also very thankful for my wife that she said, "Whatever may come upon us, this is the path that we should go!" She had never been a hindrance in this path but was ready for Jesus' sake to take any and all suffering upon ourselves. Such a helper is a gift of God!

Hardly a month had passed when a second brother stood up in the congregation, read a Bible verse and gave a short exposition of it. He was Johann Epp; today he is the leader of the congregation of Karaguj. His brother Peter Epp later became our congregational leader, and undertook to preach the Word.

There are two proverbs: "If you have lost your courage, all is lost;" and "Whoever dares, will succeed!" This is what we three experienced Johann Epp, Peter Epp, and I. We simply began to praise God and worship him; and in all of our weaknesses to exposit his Word, the Lord confirmed our service and other people came to saving faith. Ever since the years of the '30's in the Karaguj village there had not been a congregation. There were only a few old baptized Congregational members there, and these now revived, repented and set themselves to the work of faith anew. The Brethren were united in the conviction to invite some outside preachers in. Those who should be taken into the congregation, prepared their testimonies of when and how they came to the faith, and how they were now living for the Lord. Then they went out while the preachers and the other believers decided if they were really born-again and could be taken up as members.

In those first years nobody was received without the unanimous voice of the congregation. If there was even only one voice against it, then the applicant was not taken in. He would be tested examined further to see if he were well grounded. If he was not then he had to be proving himself more before he could be taken in. Some of those who had come to the faith through our ministry wanted to be baptized. Also it became clear to me that in obedience to the Word of God in Mark 16:16, that this was a Biblical sign that should follow upon the inner transformation of life. In village Number 3, which was 25 kilometers distant from us, the local congregation had dared to celebrate a baptismal meeting. This was still more dangerous than merely having a worship service. The police were always ready on the spot to hinder baptism.

With a borrowed motorcycle, I traveled to the leading Brethren of that congregation, Heinrich Esau and Johann Keller, and said to them, "I would like to become baptized." At that time there were ten other believers in our village who made application for baptism in our congregation.

Heinrich Esau was commissioned to carry out the baptisms on a July evening in the year, 1955. After the worship service we waited until the moon had disappeared behind the clouds; then we went softly for two kilometers to the Gusicha River. This was the first baptismal occasion in Karaguj since 1929. Thus, the first in 26 years. The beautiful large meetinghouse which the congregation at that time had possessed had been confiscated by the state. During the war it had been converted into a grain storage shed, later into a library, then into a dance hall. More recently (up to this day) it was being used as a mill for pressing out cooking oil. In 1978, the congregation registered itself, but it did not please the officials to give the meeting house back or give any permit for a substitute. But now God builds the congregations even without meeting houses. He can from the smallest beginnings in private houses let his people grow spiritually.

Paul writes in I Tim. 2:2, "Pray for the authorities, that we might lead a quiet and peaceable life." So just as sunshine, rain and wind are necessary in order to have a good harvest, so also the congregation of Jesus Christ needs the sunshine of peaceful rest as well as the stormy time of persecution.

In thinking of the persecution times of 1951 and '52, we were praying that the Lord would give us a time of rest. He heard us; and there followed some fruitful and peaceful years. To be sure we were visited by KGB officials and teachers, but nobody was arrested. Such visits took place especially if we had any larger gatherings or a baptismal meeting. For to such occasions many unbelievers also came. They wanted to find out why people wanted to be baptized and would put themselves in danger of persecution to make a decision for Jesus Christ. Thus, the baptismal occasions served as evangelistic opportunities. Preachers called out to the unbeliever, "Accept the Lord Jesus Christ and be converted to the living God." And it often happened that among those who were present as spectators, several were converted. This is what the officials desired to hinder in any way possible.

The kind of a total change of life which could result from such baptismal occasions, is shown in the following example. In the village of Korkino which was 1000 kilometers away, lived Wilhelm Dück. He had been a drunkard, but then was converted to God and reported to the congregational leaders that he desired to become a baptismal candidate. His former comrades in drink expected that Wasja (Wilhelm) would fall back and resume his old life with them. But they waited in vain for it. As

Wilhelm Dück was baptized at 3:00 P.M. one Sunday, four of his friends appeared at the lakeside. They saw their former comrade dressed in white baptismal clothes standing on the shore and then going into the water. Calling out they said in one voice, "Now our Wasja is lost to us!" So long as he had not been baptized they had hope that he would return with them to drinking. But now with his baptism, which they also clearly understood as a turning point, they had nothing more to hope for. Sadly they turned away.

In the summer of 1957, we had 13 applicants for baptism in our congregation. Leaders of the congregation usually set the time of baptism for the secrecy of night, or the very early morning. Only afterward was it announced at the Saturday evening or Sunday morning worship service. In this year it became possible to even have baptismal meetings in the afternoon.

Since our congregational leader Peter Epp had to work on Sunday, I was put in charge of carrying out the baptism. Among the baptismal candidates was Maria Pries, whose husband was an unbeliever and did not want her to be baptized. But he had given his permission for it just a short time before. I wanted to have a spiritual time of counsel with Maria Pries before the baptism. So I traveled on my old bicycle from the end of the village where we lived beside the road. Suddenly an auto came from the other direction. At that time there were no cars in our village. If one should happen to turn up it was a very suspicious circumstance and one thought, "Here comes the KGB to arrest somebody." As I rode my bicycle past the auto it stopped turned and drove slowly after me. A deep fear came over me. "They are after me!" I came to Gerhard Janzen's house. He stood outside and asked me, "Have you seen the car?" I answered, "Yes, but the things of God must not be allowed to go unfulfilled!" So I continued on my way and spoke with Maria Pries.

At 3:00 we gathered at Abram Dück for a short prayer meeting. Hardly had we come together, when the car drove up in front of the house. Two KGB officials and the chauffeur remained in it, but one man climbed out and came to visit the house. It was the chairman of the village council, Peter Martenow. He sat down beside me at the table on which lay a Bible and a handwritten songbook. He took them up and threw them down here and there on the table. "These books are not to be thrown around like that!" said I. Then he began to scream and shout, "Who has given you the right to hold a baptismal occasion? Who have you asked for permission?" "God's Word permits us to do it!" I answered. "I don't want to hear anything about that! Which official have you asked?" he screamed. "We have asked no officials," I said. For about ten minutes the conversation went back and forth, then he asked, "Which ones of you want to be baptized? Stand up!" Then they all stood up and gave him a testimony. Only Maria Pries remained seated, because she was not yet completely in the clear as to what she should do since her husband had been so negative. Martinow asked, "And you Maria Pries, why do you remain sitting? Don't you want to be baptized, too!" Maria Pries sat still. Then he got up and said, "I have to go! Otherwise people will say that the chairman of the village has declared himself to be a Baptist." (The word baptist is used in the USSR as a mocking word to apply to earnest believers.) After these words he went out. But we rejoiced that everything had turned out so simply, and we thanked God from our full and happy hearts.

Then we went out to the Gusiha River. As we neared the flat space on the shore which had been chosen for the baptism, we saw with astonishment that the KGB auto was already waiting there. We encouraged one another with these words: "It is God's will. He can protect us and bless us." The three KGB men and the chairman of the village stood outside the auto and called out to me, "You come here!" I went there. The one official demanded of me. "Sit here inside the auto. We want to speak with you." Hardly had I sat down in the car when they all jumped in, two of them sitting, one on either side of me, and the third took his place beside the driver. They turned on the motor, and drove away from the river.

The official beside me asked, "Are you alone going to baptize the people? Or is another one ready to do this?" I simply answered, "I'm the only one in charge of this; it is God's work and nobody can stop this work. If you kidnap me, God will choose another Brother, or even a whole row of Brethren, who will spring up as substitutes for me. I have no idea whom he will use for this work today!" But I could name a number of persons who would be able to do it. As out of one mouth the KGB officials shouted to the driver, "Halt!" We were about 400 meters distant now from the baptismal place. The auto stood there. The three officials got out and consulted with one another outside. I could hear nothing of what they said. But concerning what the driver told me I was very astonished. "Hopefully they will baptize them quickly so that it will already be done when we drive back!" He probably was on our side in his own heart. Meanwhile the discussion outside ended. They opened the door and demanded of me, "Get out! You stay here with one official! We both will drive back." And immediately they roared away.

I said to the official who stood beside me. "I'm not going to stay here! I'm going back to the stream and we are going to complete that baptism. And then you can bring me where you want! Immediately I made the first step toward the stream. "You're not going there! You remain here!" called the official. Now I began to run and the official could not overtake me. As I came to the place of baptism, the service had already begun and Johann Epp was at the point of starting the baptizing. The three officials commanded him to get in the auto with them. But he was more suspicious than I and would not do it. He stepped calmly into the water and the candidates for baptism followed him. One of the KGB called out, "Epp, get out of that water! Come here!" But he would not do it, and the KGB officials could do nothing. They did not want to go into the water because that would ruin their beautiful suits. So they had to watch as spectators as the baptismal candidates were baptized. Even Maria Pries was baptized despite her having remained silent to the question put to her by the village chairman.

The Lord gave us a special joy. Five of the spectators declared before the congregation that they also wanted to believe in the Lord Jesus Christ. Then our songs of praise and thanksgiving, and songs to the Lord ascended on high. After that, we dismissed those present with a short admonition. We hastened away because we had reckoned that the KGB officials who had retreated, may have gone to bring reinforcements and some of the Brethren would be arrested. However they did not come back. This was a result of God's gracious protection.

Chapter 3

Denunciation And Threats

To be sure the KGB official soon left, but I found out later that they demanded of the collective farm chief that I should be fired from my work—charge of the pigs. But no one else wanted this kind of work because it stank so frightfully in the pig stalls. If anyone would come in there, it would only be by holding his nose and mouth shut and seeking to get out as quickly as possible. We workers in the pig stalls had become accustomed to stench. Often we had to spend several days and even nights in the stalls, and even take our meals there, if the sows were having little pigs so that the little ones would not be smothered.

On the Monday after the baptismal celebration, the sun shone as brightly as on Sunday and my heart was full of joy over the fact that nobody had been arrested. I wanted to go into a store in order to buy something. Then I saw on the door of the store a poster which pictured swine with open mouths standing on their back legs as though they were crying for feed. Beside the swine one could see the drawing of a man kneeling. Then I thought to myself: "Is that supposed to be me and my swine?" Under the illustration there was an article. As I read it everything became clear to me. I was accused as though I had busied myself with the Christian faith and carried out a baptismal celebration on Sunday, while in the meantime I had neglected the swine in an irresponsible manner so that they had to stand up on their hind legs and scream for feed. On these grounds, the poster demanded that my work be taken from me. These were all pure lies. Actually, I had successfully raised most of the little pigs from the sows that had been entrusted to me. While other workers on the contrary had lost many of their little pigs. For this reason I was supposed to receive a reward—a pig of seventy kilograms and with it two young piglets. The large pig I did receive, but the two little piglets were withheld from me.

I did not raise any objections to this, but said to myself, "If this happens for Jesus' sake, then let it be so. We already have enough to eat and our necessary clothes and we will be content with those things." The Lord Jesus says in Matthew 5:11-12, "Blessed are ye when men shall revile you and persecute you, and shall say all manner of evil against you falsely for my sake. Rejoice and be exceeding glad: for great is your reward in heaven: …" Eight months later I did get one of those little pigs which I had earned as a prize. It was now springtime and the piglet was worth much more than the two piglets that I should have received in the autumn. Peter Unger, the controller, had seen to it that I got what I had coming to me. Although he was not a believer, he was a person who tried to do what is just.

On Tuesday the wife of Peter Derksen came and said to me, "I'm supposed to take over your swine." On Wednesday accordingly I went to the place by the horse barn where the work was divided up. Now it was decided that I would be sent into carpentry. How glad I was about that! Now I could come home earlier in the evenings, and on Sundays I would not need to go out working, so I could regularly go to the worship services. And in addition, I could now always go out into the fresh air. However, that lasted for only three months, for in the swine stalls it just did not go well without my presence. The collective farm chief came to me and said, "It was a mistake that we have taken you away from this work. But this was commanded by those who are above us. Come again to your former work!" So that is what I had to do then.

Six years passed by since I had begun in my weakness to preach. For five years now our congregation stood, and many people had come to the faith and been baptized. Where spiritual life is, there is also struggle. For the enemy of our souls does not sleep. Sometimes there were persecutions from the state, then again there were difficulties between the Brethren of the congregation. Where sin is not called sin, or even patiently tolerated, there is peace and calm, but it is like a cemetery. But when congregation discipline is used, the old nature rises up to contradict it. There were Brethren who thought that one must overlook faults. They justified themselves in this position through the words in I Peter 4:8 "Love covers a multitude of sins." But this opinion we could not share. We did not want to suffer evil and we busied ourselves to help the members of the church to lead a holy life. From this came many a struggle.

The officials had not arrested any of us in these six years. However, at the end of this time, 1959, we were sharply attacked once again, and commanded to stop preaching. Most sharply the KGB threatened Peter Epp and me, because we had continued unmoved to preach the Word of God and to baptize believing men. But we did not let ourselves be frightened because the Bible does not allow us to be silent about the Gospel. However, as the threats became more and more frequent, then we had to think of the words of Jesus in Matthew 10:23, "When they persecute you in one city, then flee into another." We counseled with the members of the church and they said, "It is probably the best thing for you to move away at this point. The best that we would desire would be to keep you here." So now both of us, Peter Epp and I, planned to move 2300 kilometers away with our families, to the region of Frunze not far from the Chinese border.

Again and again we were summoned to hearings and threatened. Fear crept into our hearts. Many times our knees shook. But as soon as I sat on the chair in front of the Communists, I became completely calm. During one of the hearings my knees would not stop trembling, although my heart was still. I didn't want the officials to see that my knees were trembling. So I grabbed my knees with both hands and said in my thoughts: "Now finally, you be still!" How glad I was that the Lord had given me this thought! After that I could calmly reply to all the questions and not implicate any of the other Brethren.

First the KGB people tried a friendly tactic, "How's it going now with your work? Are you earning enough to support your family well?" Then more dangerous questions were put to me: "Where were you on Sunday? Who preached?" They tried in every possible way to move me to say something that would implicate other Brethren. Then they would call someone else to the hearing and ask them about me and the other Brethren. In this way they tried to set us against one another. I said nothing about the other Brethren, however, and only spoke about my own experience with God. This they did not want to hear about and they began to scold and to rage and to curse. Soon they began to threaten to send me and my family to some other region of Russia.

During another hearing there were four officials working against me alone. They screamed and cursed. Suddenly three of them went out, and one remained with me. Why the three went out I do not know. But I was now afraid of what they were going to do with me next. I prayed in my heart, "Lord, thou art with me. And let happen whatever is according to your will."

The official who had remained behind in the room with me had a lame leg and had to go about with a cane. Since I would say nothing against the other Brethren, he became furious and struck against the table in a rage so that it made a loud crack. At first I thought he wanted to beat me, but I remained calm and asked in a friendly tone, "Are you a Communist? And do you belong to the party?" Furiously he answered, "That has nothing to do with you!" I asked another time but he gave no answer. Then I said, "This is not the way Communists treat believers. To pound against the table is not their way. They want to convince the believers with reasonable grounds, and persuade them over with good. So at least your periodicals say." "With you nobody can speak reasonably," said he. Then he wanted to know which of the Brethren were preaching. However I named no other Brother because it would be a mistake to do so, as some had done in earlier hearings. That was because we did not at that time know the techniques of the KGB who always tried to get us to involve other people. I had thought at that time, "Everybody really knows who is preaching so I can calmly say these names to the KGB. But they know well how to use even harmless expressions and admissions concerning the other Brethren for evil purposes. If the Brethren, for example, would only sometimes be mentioned in each hearing this would soon add up to a regular case against them, and cause them more anxiety and fear. For this reason I had undertaken never again to mention another name. But to lie was out of the question. I did, however, have the possibility to remain silent in order to bring no danger to anyone.

Gradually the excited official calmed himself again. Then the other three officials returned. I preferred that. For if one is present with only one other person, he can make up things and pretend that one has said things because there are no witnesses present.

At this hearing it became clear to me that they were seeking a case against Peter Epp and myself in order to have us arrested. The officials asked me if Brother Epp and I were planning to move away with our families. Then they said, "That will never be allowed. First we will prove whether or not you have spoken against the law of the land in your congregation. And then, you will not come into the warm region of Frunze but we will send you to the ice cold region of northern Siberia, because your case is full and ready to be dealt with! And as I left the room, Peter Epp was called in to be interrogated.

At home I spoke with my wife. We were united together in our determination. "We will not let ourselves be driven away from our faith, and the

Gospel must continue to be preached no matter what happens to us." We discussed whether we should not, for sake of security, change our worship services to other days and meet at other times. Also we could use birthdays, weddings and burials as an opportunity for preaching the Gospel. But to be silent about the Word of God as the Communists officials desired, was against God's will and our conscience. We wanted to live alone by the Word of God.

I owned half of a Bible at that time, which I had received shortly before my conversion and out of which I preached for ten years (from 1948 to 1958). It contained the 25th chapter of Proverbs and the New Testament. My wife also had parts of the Bible which she brought to our home at our marriage, and her's included the Old Testament with some epistles of the New Testament. Thus, together we possessed somewhat more than a whole single Bible and felt ourselves to be unutterably rich. In the Soviet Union very few people possess a complete Bible. For example, in 1956, our congregation received a letter from Taschkent, about 200 kilometers away from us. The congregation there wrote that they only had the Psalms, and begged us to send to them some other part of the Holy Scriptures. Accordingly we pooled whatever we could find in our congregation. It became clear to my wife and I that we could not keep two half Bibles when the group at Taschkent had only the Psalms. After a short discussion we were united to resolve to send my wife's half of the Bible to Taschkent. And over there great joy reigned because of this gift.

Chapter 4

Comrades' Court

Almost daily we leading Brethren of the congregation were hauled in for hearings. What they had in mind for us, was never told to us. We suspected that we would be placed before a court and condemned. The congregation stood true and faithfully behind us in these critical days, with encouragement and intercessions. It was announced that on the 23rd and 24th of February, 1960, a fellow-worker's court would meet in the community building of our district. The fellow-worker's court is composed of fellow workers of the collective farm. We were full of heavy thoughts. Will the hard times of '51 and '52 come again with many arrests? From our congregation the seven leading Brethren were summoned: Peter Epp, Johann Epp, Dietrich Janzen, Gerhard Janzen, Peter Lietke, Peter Berge and I. Otherwise, none of our congregation was there. But at this time all of the leading personnel of the the seven villages of our collective farm were summoned to come on horse sleds, the officials, the party men, the teachers, etc. In the front on the stage sat the men of the official committees and the KGB men.

The trial began with desolate scoldings and shoutings and lasted all five hours long. We believers were accused of being bad citizens of the Soviet Union, traitors of our people, enemies of progress, and opponents of socialism. It was said that our children were being trained to be spiritual cripples, because we filled them full of dangerous Christian teachings, instead of raising them to be useful to the communistic ideals. Our men should stop preaching this foolishness, and be spending their time on productive work. The leaders of the officials constantly agitated the spectators and poured oil on the fire. The crowd became raging; and shouted: "Away with them! Punish them! Send them to northern Siberia! They don't deserve to live!" It was frightful to be in this witche's caldron of hatred. But this evening also passed by. We breathed freely as we went out into the fresh air of God's world.

The next evening it was supposed to continue on. And this time all the believers were invited; also those of the Mennonite congregation with their preachers.

A new nurse who was among the spectators, didn't know what was going on and asked the question publicly what it was that we had preached. As good as I could I started to answer. But then I was interrupted by one of the officials, "He is going to start to preach here too!"

Then it was required that we Brethren come to the front and declare: "We will not hold any meetings! We will not preach any more! And we will deny the faith!" Only one man went up to the stage and declared out loud, "I herewith deny all belief in God!" Some others, however, promised that they would not preach anymore if the authorities did not allow it. Another man was asked: "Will you continue to speak from the Bible if anyone comes to visit you?" he said, "No! I will never do that again!" Then an old teacher stood up. He did not really belong to the believers, but he said before us all; "Those here who have promised to say nothing more from the Bible, have made themselves guilty before God and men! I have studied from childhood about religion and I know that it is the duty and the holy task of all believers to share the Gospel with all men. When these here deny that, they have made themselves guilty; as I have said, they have made themselves guilty before God and men!"

My heart ached that some of the Brethren had given themselves over to the slippery way of unbelief, and I could have wept. Then I stood up without any permission and said to one of them, "You listen to me! Take back what you have said! The old teacher has told us how we have to act!" Then there arose a fearful shouting: "Hold your mouth! We don't want to hear that! How can we have any patience with such people any longer. Away with them to the far North; and there they can pray with the polar bears!"

We were astonished, however, over the mild conclusion of the comrades' court which only resulted in a warning! "If any of you gather together to preach, then we will undertake a sharp action against you. (The comrades' court could not legally deliver a public punishment except for warnings, monitary fines of 50 rubles at the most, or it could turn the matter over to the state prosecuting attorney). At midnight the whole case was at an end. How often we had been threatened. But our God held his protecting hand over us. Some Brethren who had backslidden, were once again converted, but some were not. God knows their heart and their end, and he is the just judge.

10. A group of the youth attending the wedding of the oldest daughter Maria Hamm, with Cornelius Martens, in 9-12-73, at Iwanowka.

Chapter 5

Moving To Kirghiz

On the next day — it was the 25th of February, 1960-Peter Epp and I traveled with our families at sunset to Frunze. We had already long since had everything packed in the event that we would have to flee to Frunze. Since it was very cold, we had prepared a large tractor drawn sled with a super-structure made of wood and covered by a large tarp so that we together with our total of nine children could sit inside of it as in a hut. We had placed a wood heated oven inside of it plus a good supply of wood and coal.

Many believers stood in the street. They rejoiced with us that we would be able to travel to such a warm region. But they also wept because they would have gladly kept us with them. With anxious faces turned toward the heavens, everyone noticed that a strong snowstorm was setting in. Soon the landscape together with the road would be completely covered so that it would be difficult for us to find our way. Through the whole night we would have to heat the stove because it had become so cold. As soon as it was dawn, we drove finally into Orenburg and came to the railroad station. On the third floor of the railroad building there was a room for women with children. And there we brought our wives and children. We now had nine hours to wait until our train would leave.

Peter Epp and I now had the problem before us of securing a container in which we could pack all our belongings. This container stood on the other side of the railroad station. And the crane which would be necessary to move it over to our side was not functioning. It was already early afternoon when we finally located a suitable container. Now we had to hurry because at 5 o'clock our train was scheduled to depart. The women waited and waited in vain on us, until they finally had to go to the train

themselves. Then they experienced the friendly grace of God. He gave
the women officials compassion for these wives with their many children
so that they helped them to pick up their suitcases, and they led the group
by a sheltered way to the platform. In this manner they did not need to join
the long rows of waiting people. My wife said to the older children Maria
and Jacob, "Hold on fast to each others hands. You Maria, take the coffee
can, and you Jacob the sack with the night jar. Go behind our aunt here."
My wife took Cathrine by the hand, and with the other hand she held on
the travel cradle on one end. The other end was supported by a girl so that
this could be taken with us too. She went across the great courtyard to the
railroad station door. And there she remained standing for a moment. A
woman official asked her teasingly, "Are all your children here?" and
smiled when she said it. Both of the women answered, "Yes, they are all
here!" They really believed they were, but then my wife looked over the
group of children and said, "Oh my dear! Maria is missing! Stay here, I
will go back and look for Maria!"

She hurried back, and in her excitement she ran right by Maria. What
was happening then? In the middle of the railroad station square there
stood a great monument to Stalin. Maria had never seen any such thing
before so she stayed there gawking at the enormous monument. When she
wanted to go on again nobody was to be seen of our group. So then she
began to scream and to cry with the loudest voice she could, "Mama!
Mama!" But no mama was to be seen anywhere. Immediately a policeman came and asked her in Russian, "Where then is your mama?" Maria
did not understand Russian. So she began to scream even louder;
"Mama! Mama!" A few other travelers happened to have noticed how
two women with many children had gone by and said to the policeman,
"Some ladies with many children went over in this direction. Surely they
went to the train which is just about to arrive. Perhaps this child belongs
to them." Then the policeman took the girl by the hand and said, "Come
with me, and we will look for your mama!" In the same minute my wife
ran by and because of her great excitement did not even see her child.
Fortunately Maria began to cry miserable at that moment, "Mama!
Mama!" This was heard by her mother and she hurried over and seized
Maria by the hand saying, "Ah, my child there you are! Where have you
been?" "Now you see your mama has found you again!" And he told the
mother what had happened with her child. The mother was very cheerful
but now the train had arrived and the female attendant helped them in.
Everyone found a place, but now the two men were still missing.

Peter Epp and I had just finished with the packing of the container, and only the lead seals were missing on it. In spite of cold and snowflurries, sweat stood on our faces. Finally along came a conductor who put the lead seals on the container. We both ran as fast as we could to the train. The locomotive whistled signaling its departure as we reached it and jumped on. Immediately it departed. We waved to our brother-in-law who had accompanied us and then we sat down in our places. We were completely out of breath and our hearts were beating mightly. Only after a long time could we calm ourselves.

Then we took our song books out and began to sing cheerful praise and thanksgiving hymns and songs. From the other compartments travelers came and rushed over to us. They were astonished that we would be traveling in such bad winter weather with so many children.

After a time the train was traveling through a wilderness. We could see white patches of sand, little huts, and also camels and donkeys. After 36 hours journey we came to a place called Aress, where we had to get out and change trains. Here already it was wonderfully warm just like in summer—no snow, no winter. We felt very good. The children jumped around in the sunshine like little lambs. The overseer of this railroad station and a doctor laughed to see what fun the children were having. We had to spend 36 hours in this station. The next day at 6:30 P.M. we climbed on the next train which would bring us to Iwanoka in Kirgisien.

The relatives of Peter Epp picked us up at the train station, and drove us to their little house. We could not all stay in it because it was too small. A believing man by the name of Cornelius Harder took me with my family to his home. To be sure he had only a small earthen hut with a kitchen and one bedroom, but we all laid down in a row on the earthen floor and were cheerful and satisfied, to find ourselves among loving people for the next ten days.

Sometime later we received a letter from friends in Orenburg in which they wrote us that the KGB officials had come to the collective farm head and asked, "Why have you let them escape?"

We had made a covenant with the family of Peter Epp that we would always stay together. But we were also prepared to live in whatever place to which God would lead us. It was, however, not easy to know the will of God. Always and again we prayed for him to show us the way. However, we received no assurance from him that we should move anywhere else. My wife and I finally realized that we should remain in Iwanowka. For 1500 rubles we bought a small cottage and a milk goat, wherewith we

would be able to have milk for our children. We had to spend the whole
summer repairing and remodeling the little cottage we had bought. But at
least it was something that belonged to us. I soon found work in a sawmill
as a watchman; but wages and food were very scarce at that time.

My wife and I asked to be taken up among the unregistered Mennonite
Church. It was a Mennonite Brethren congregation, at that place whose
elder was Jacob Peters. We gave our testimony to the congregation as to
how we had come to faith in Jesus Christ, and then we were taken up. The
meeting house was only a very poor little earthen hut. Later, the walls
were raised somewhat and a thicker earth roof was put on top of it. Also
larger windows were set in the wall so that we would have more light inside. But we could not enjoy it very long for in the summer of 1960, KGB
officials came and forbade our gathering together, locking up the earthen
hut. Then we divided ourselves in three groups and met together in private houses.

One evening in the summer of 1962, we celebrated a memorable baptismal occasion beside the great canal. After that Jacob Peters was called
in for court hearing. It was thrown up to him that he had supposedly gathered people together in private houses which is forbidden by the government. He replied, "But you have taken away our meeting house, so now
where should we gather ourselves?" The answer came back, "Nowhere,
not at all!" Further, he was accused of arranging a baptismal celebration
and that even in public. But it was not really a public occasion, for it happened in the evening and secretly. Finally, he was accused of going into
various houses agitating against the government to persuade parents that
they could not let their children join the pioneers (which was the communist youth group). With this he was supposed to have revealed himself to
be an enemy of the Soviet State.

We should explain that many believers of our congregation did not want
their children to wear the red neckscarf of pioneers, because this was a
sign of atheism. However, many other congregations, on the contrary,
gladly let their children wear the red neckscarves and belong to the pioneers, for they believe that Romans 13 required us to obey the authorities.
They also claimed at that time that they believed since the children were
very young, they were really not responsible. It did so happen that later
many of the youth that came to Jesus Christ, became converted and lived
a good Christian life even though they had earlier belonged to the pioneers and wore the red neck scarf. Children however, who did not belong
to the state youth group had a very hard time in school. They were often

scolded, and fellow students were set upon them to beat them. They found no assistance from the teachers, for they looked the other way in order to be able to say that they had not seen anything.

Since we in our congregation did not want our children to belong to the communist youth group the officials raged against us. In September of 1962, Jacob Peters was arrested. And in November of 1962, he was sentenced to four years in a concentration camp. In May of 1965, he was rehabilitated, declared innocent and released. As so called compensation he received two months wages, or the equivalent of 120 rubles. From then on we came together only secretly, and in small groups. Whoever found it possible, purchased a radio and listened to the Russian programs broadcasted from Monte Carlo in France with evangelical programs. Also I could purchase a radio at this time, and we invited believers and unbelievers alike to come into our house while we closed the windows and put up the curtains and listened to God's Word. Through that we were not only consoled and edified, but it came about some people were led to living faith in Christ. After a time some brethren again found courage and we began to meet together with the Brothers and Sisters in three groups in private houses.

9. The family of Abram Hamm in the year 1971 without the father, because at this time he was serving his second term in prison.

Chapter 6

A New House For Us And For The Congregation In Iwanowka

The following song we often sang at that time:
> Time is hurrying on,
>   And we, we must hurry with her.
> No standing still here,
>   No rest, no stalling of time ...

So one year after another passed by and our family kept getting larger, but our little cottage did not grow along with it. My wife and I deliberated together as to whether we should build another house or not. My wife was holding back somewhat. But I had the courage to do it. We prayed, "Lord Jesus we would like to build a house for you and for us." That is to say we not only wanted room and space for our own family but also enough for the worship service groups of our congregation.

The collective farm granted us a lot of 800 square meters. We did not have to pay anything at all for it except for yearly taxes, because in the USSR no land is actually sold by anyone. I spread clay with a bulldozer on the construction site. We had enough straw left from the winter, and water ran in a small ditch nearby. We had no money, but we borrowed as much as we thought was necessary. Then when we were able to sell the house in which we lived to that point, we would be able to pay back the borrowed money.

My wife and I were the contractors, the laborers, and the skilled artisans at the same time. Since we were healthy, had faith and courage enough, the work went forward wonderfully well. So that my wife could even more valiantly help with this work, my mother came from Orenburg to take care of our children.

Sundays of course we did not work but held our worship services and

in the construction. By October, 1963, we were celebrating our firs
Thanksgiving in our own house.

After Jacob Peters had been convicted in September, 1962, the congre
gation had chosen Peter Petger as the Elder. Heinrich Esau was chosen a
his helper; I was appointed as youth leader and also entrusted with th
children's groups. We had divided the children into age groups of 8-1
year olds and 12-14 year olds, and then those that were older. More an
more people came to believe and were baptized. Gradually it became ap
parent to us we needed a larger space for our gatherings. Then we hear
that the congregation at Nowopawlowka near Frunze had built a beautifu
tabernacle in which the whole congregation could assemble. We also de
cided to build such a tabernacle. Of course it was not very fancy, mor
like a shed of wood with a wooden canvas top.

In the summer of 1965, we began to erect it near our house which lay a
the end of the street. The land actually belonged to the collective farm bu
was not used for any agricultural purpose. Members of the congregatio
put used wood to use in this construction, plus other wood that we wer
able to buy, and all could be cut and shaped with a circular saw. We wer
all of great courage and enthusiasm as we went about this work.

Soon the walls of the tabernacle were up. Only the roof was not ye
ready. Since it was still good weather we decided to hold a Thanksgivin
service in our new tabernacle. But then some officials of the governmen
came along and demanded to know, "Who has given you permission t
build here? We are going to smash this whole thing down with a bull
dozer!" When I came home from work and found out about this I said t
my wife, "When the bulldozer comes, you take our daughter (Anna tw
years old) in your arms and place yourself in front of the bulldozer. Th
driver will not drive you over." My wife naturally experienced great anxi
ety and we prayed about it so that the Lord would protect her. Actually th
bulldozer never arrived.

We brethren now deliberated as to what was the best course to take. Ou
elder, Peter Petger, made the proposal. "We could rebuild the tabernacl
in my garden. No one can forbid us to do it there because I have the use o
this land for my whole life and each year I have been paying taxes on it.'
So this is what happened. We quickly disassembled the tabernacle
loaded it on a wagon and dragged it with a tractor to Petger's house. In hi
garden we erected it once again. An electrician quickly wired it for lights
We were able to rejoice that the whole congregation could assembl
themselves to worship God in one space with good lighting!

Chapter 7

A Youth Meeting And Its Consequences

In the USSR it is the custom for believers to have a youth meeting between the 1st and 2nd of May, or between the 7th and 8th of November, which is called the Octoberfest. We youth leaders from the Frunza district planned such a youth conference in Iwanowka for the 8th of November, 1965; but this date could only be made known the day before. We had made all the preparations and then invited the youth groups to present their song, poetry and music. None-the-less the KGB heard about it and on the 7th of November G. Klassen and I were summoned for a hearing. The officials spoke very sharply with us and said, "If this youth conference for the Frunza district takes place among you, then you can start toasting bread and stacking it up!" (That means: "Then we are going to put you in prison.") They didn't make many words! From experience we knew that when they speak much, nothing much is to be feared; but when they speak little, they are going to take action. On the next morning I traveled with my bicycle to our elder and asked him, "What will we do now? Should we postpone the youth meeting?" He replied, "The guests are invited, whoever comes let him come and whoever does not come is not worthy!" So we let it remain that way. All the youth groups except one came. The leading Brethren of the Nowopawlowka congregation were afraid and did not allow their youth to come to us. They hoped by that to be able to save their pavilion, or tabernacle, but their calculation was incorrect. A few days later their tabernacle was destroyed by the officials. Our tabernacle, to the contrary, stood for another eight months longer.

Already early in the morning of November 8th, youth from all sides streamed to our tabernacle. Hardly had we begun with our youth confer-

145

ence when up drove a bus and two passenger vans with KGB people. They called us Brethren outside and said, "Yesterday we commanded you that you should not carry out this youth conference. Tomorrow morning early, at 9:00 o'clock, you are to be present at a hearing in Tokmak!" But they did not drive us apart from each other nor arrest us; but at that time they just drove away. We thanked God that we could continue to have our youth meeting. Some of the youth made a decision for Jesus Christ and all of the participants were encouraged anew.

After the youth conference, I had to take my wife to the hospital because a child was expected. This was our Lydia. I prayed with my wife and laid everything in God's hands. I said to my wife, "It is possible that I will not return from tomorrow's hearing; but will be arrested." She answered, "However God rules, we will accept it!" I rejoiced and was thankful that my wife was of one mind with me.

I hurried the next day to Tokmak to the hearing. Because of my visit to the hospital I was somewhat late. Some of the Brethren were already finished with their hearings. As it came to my turn I was asked immediately, "Why have you not heeded the orders of the officials and went ahead to hold your conference?" I answered, "One must obey God rather than men!" As I gazed at the officials, I noted that these were other people than those who had spoken to us on the preceding days. That was good, for these would not know exactly all the details about the youth conference. A KGB female official said to me, "There were also some youth in your tabernacle. You know that is not allowed!" I thought to myself you don't really know the facts, for there were *only* youth present at the youth conference (besides us ministers)." Then she warned me that we should stop carrying on such activities. I remained quiet and then I was permitted to go.

The other Brethren experienced much the same thing. We were all astonished at the wonderful leading of God. Just when we think we are at the end, then God is just beginning his work!

In that warm region of Frunza, winter was exceptionally mild. However, even in the few days in which it was really cold, we came together regularly in our little tabernacle, and scattered a thick layer of sawdust on the floor so that our feet would be warmer. In the course of the worship services it always became warmer yet, because so many people — usually about 300-were present. The communist officials summoned us Brethren again and again and demanded of us that we break up our tabernacle. Some thought that we should do it because of Romans 13 where he says we should respect the authorities who are over us. But our elder Peter Petger answered, "We have not built this tabernacle to tear it down, but to preach the Gospel in it!"

One day we came to our tabernacle, and found that we could not get into it, for the police had locked it up. Then Peter Petger lifted his little son up to the roof and the boy crept across the roof until he could reach a little window which was set in the roof for ventilation. He swung into this window, and down to the floor of the tabernacle and then opened the second door which was only barred from within. So we could continue with our worship service after all.

Now the KGB officials tried other measures to try to block our growing congregation. They demanded of us that we should be registered so that we would be officially recognized. But it was well known to us that registered congregations were much more restricted in their movements. They did not dare to have any children's or youth work, and they did not dare to evangelize, and they did not dare to print Bibles nor distribute them. Women's work, visits from house to house, and welfare work were forbidden. But we did not want to allow ourselves to be restricted in these ways.

Meanwhile our congregation had grown to 250 members, and seventeen of us belonged to the ministerial council now. There we discussed the question: "What does the Word of God say about this demand? Can we accept upon ourselves these restrictions?" We had before us for study an application form for registration and we saw that we could answer all the questions with a good conscience except one. This one question gave us great sorrow. It was whether we would be ready to agree with and comply with the law governing religious cults. This law contained within it the above mentioned restrictions. But we would only be ready to let ourselves be registered if the officials would not interfere with our congregational work.

During this time we received a visit from Woschtschuk, who at that time was the ruling elder of the entire province for all denominations, that is in the Kasach and Kirgisian SSR. He was responsible for all the registered congregations in this district. He attempted to persuade us that it would not be so bad to sign up for registration. Many congregations had already allowed themselves to be registered and we did not need to fear that our work would be restricted as much as it sounded. He implied that we would allow ourselves to be restricted, but we could go ahead and do what we wanted to do anyway. That did not seem right to us to sign something with reservations in our mind and then not carry it out. Jesus Christ said plainly, "Let your speech be 'Yes, yes, and no, no,' what is more than this is from evil. (Matt. 5:37)

Woschtschuk remained for an entire week in our congregation and sought to persuade us that everything would not be so bad if we would only allow ourselves to be registered. Our elder Peter Petger and another Brother said, "We cannot do such a thing with a clear conscience! We would defile our consciences." To start with, all seventeen Brethren were of the same opinion. But after a week of Woschtschuk's persuasion, the picture changed and finally half the Brethren voted to adopt his opinion. So there arose in our congregation a split; especially after Peter Petger's arrest in July of 1966. Two-thirds of our congregation were ready to let the church be registered. The remnant of us, however, gathered together in private houses and did not fail to have a single worship service. The others however, who trusted in the promises of the KGB that as soon as they would be a registered congregation they could meet as often as they wanted, agreed that they should not gather together until their registration was received from the government. So for almost two months they did not gather together. And still they did not receive their registration. Then some of them became restless, and said, "That will never do. Who knows how long we will have to give up our meetings and still not receive our registration. Let's meet together again!" For almost 10 long years they had to wait until they were finally registered. Meanwhile, they did not have any more close fellowship with us.

Between the Brethren of the registered congregation and our unregistered congregation this question of registration always came up. Again and again it was discussed and it led to differences. The Brethren of the registered congregation were ready to take upon themselves the restrictions the government had put on evangelistic work, because of Romans 13, and our supposed duty to always obey the authorities. They threw it up to us that we were beating our heads against the wall. But we held it up to them that Romans 13 did not say we are responsible to an atheistic government to put rules on our internal congregational life. In fact, we could not permit it to be done because the command of Jesus is to preach the Gospel to all men. In cases like this we must follow Acts 5:29 — We must obey God rather than men.

No other passage of the Bible was so much expounded and disputed among us at that time as Romans 13. Because we were not an officially tolerated congregation, even the godless officials constantly threw it up to us that we were disobedient to the Word of God according to Romans 13.

According to Romans 13:3 we should really have received praise from the governmental authorities because we were not doing anything evil but only following our duty conscientiously. Day and night we worked hard to the point of exhaustion. Even on Sundays we were not given much rest or leisure by the officials.

In June of 1956, I received vacation leave and tried to take a round trip with a stop-over in Moscow where I might be able to secure a Bible. In the worship services of the Baptists in Moscow, I saw several foreigners, including a few Africans, and saluted them with a firm handshake. Since we did not know one another's languages, this handshake and our cheerful faces had to express that we were all the children of God. Two ladies from Holland were also present and I began a conversation with them in Plattdeutsch. I asked them if they might not have brought a Russian Bible with them. But unfortunately they had already given all their Bibles to the leading Brethren of the Moscow congregation.

But among their group there was a third lady from Holland and to her I said, "I still do not have a Russian Bible. Could you give me one?" I have a Russian Bible but it is at my hotel. Since I had to shortly leave on a flight to Lithuania, I could not go with her to her hotel. I explained to her that the following Wednesday I would be back in Moscow again and visit this worship service. "That is good," said she, "Come with me now to this Brother over here. We went to him and she said to him, "I have a Russian Bible. I will give it to you and you give it next Wednesday to this man here!" Thereby she pointed to me. Full of heartfelt thanks I absented myself.

As I came the following Wednesday from Lithuania back to Moscow, the train was held up and I was late so I had to hurry and run from the station to the bus stop. After the bus trip I still had to go a portion on foot before I could reach this church meeting. I ran as fast as I could and people stared at me. But that was all the same to me. I was thinking only: "I've got to have that Bible! The Russian Bible!" Finally I reached the meeting house only to find the people streaming out of it. I looked at the many men and wondered which one is it that is supposed to give me the Bible? It was going through my head, "Will I be able to find him or not." Then suddenly one of the men spoke to me, "Ah-ha, you're the one! I've been looking and looking and couldn't see you in the worship service. But now everything is alright. Here is your Bible!" How glad I was and I thanked him heartily. Then I had to hurry back to continue my journey to the railroad station.

During the return journey I visited my mother and relatives in the Orenberger District. There I received a telegram from my wife, "Come home immediately!" What can that mean? I thought. Is one of the children sick, or has one died? If so, she surely would have mentioned that. If the house is burned down, I can't help it any if I come home earlier. With some unrest I turned myself back toward's my homeward journey. During the last part of the journey I met an acquaintance from our village who asked, "Don't you know what has happened among us?" "No," said I. Then he told me, "The Comrade officials court met and decided to arrest three persons and give them over for punishment; Peter Petger, G. Klassen and yourself. Our tabernacle has been broken down. The police arrested Peter Petger while he was at work. He had to stand by and watch while the soldiers smashed our tabernacle with a bulldozer and wrecking bars. At the end, everything was loaded onto big trucks and carried away. Petger and G. Klassen were taken away immediately afterwards. If you would have been at home, there you would have also been arrested. It will not be long now before they will come and fetch you."

When I reached home I learned the same thing from my wife. We were resigned that I would soon be arrested. The short time that remained to me I wanted to use to visit the families of the two arrested brethren and console them. On the next day I visited first the Klassen family. I could hardly understand why G. Klassen himself had already returned home. But he had purchased his freedom by making an agreement with the authorities which was not in accord with God's will. He had promised not to do any children's or youth work in connection with worship services. This he confessed to me immediately. Two days of arrest had succeeded in causing him to give in. We prayed together and thanked God for his liberation. But my heart was sad. Then I hurried to the Petger family. The father of the house was not at home, but had to remain in investigative arrest. This made it clear to me that he had given a clear testimony and was not moved from the decision to follow his Lord.

Chapter 8

Court Case Against Peter Petger

The next morning, it was Monday; and I had to go away to work with a construction brigade which was in construction in a place some 35 kilometers distant. We usually left on Monday mornings and came back on Saturday. So on the following Saturday when I came home my wife reported that on Tuesday the police had been there in order to fetch me. One month went by and I remained free. Then came a summons to a court hearing in the town of Tokmak, 25 kilometers distant. I traveled there but did not meet the state attorney. They told me that I should go back to my village of Iwanowka where he would see me. At home I did not meet him either, and for that reason I went back again to my work. During the next fourteen days I remained unmolested. During this time witnesses against Peter Petger were sought among the believers. Even my nine year old daughter was questioned in school whether she went to the children's worship service, and whether Peter Petger had instructed her. Her answers were written up and she had to sign them. This was learned only later.

The case was scheduled for October, 1966. I was astonished that my daughter Kathrina also had a summons to appear. I asked her, "Tina, did you sign something in school?" "Yes, our teacher, Anna Nikolajewna had taken me into the teacher's room. There was an older man who asked me many questions. Then the teacher said, "Sign your name here! And that I did." "But Tina, why did you do that?" I asked. "Father, you always told us that we should obey the teachers in everything. Only when he would say that there is no God or when he would mock about God and say such things as that I should not believe, that then I should not cooperate." Against this I could say nothing. But what the school had done was an open assault against the laws of the land which said that an innocent child could not be questioned without the presence of his parents. But in any case the officials did with the believers what they wanted to do even if they trampled their own laws under foot.

If the case had been handled as planned in Tokmak, then very few people out of our settlement would have been able to take part as spectators. But they wanted as many believers as possible to be present and to be intimidated. For this reason the court case was changed to meet in the dance club of Iwanowka. Many people streamed into the room: the believers out of sympathy, and the unbelievers out of curiosity or the desire to see someone punished. My wife and I both went. We wanted to see how Peter Petger would be handled. His face was pale and his figure thin but his eyes glowed with friendliness. Many of the believing ladies wept when they saw him. Peter Petger remained calm and selfcontained. My wife and I did not cry because shortly before Peter's arrest he and I had both spoken to our wives and promised: "If we are taken before the court may God give the grace that we do not need to cry." We were thankful that God granted us this strength to be completely calm and content.

The court case began and the witnesses were called, even my daughter Katrina. But she was not there. When I showed her the summons and said to her, "You have signed something with your name in school. Now they want you to stand before the court judge and testify against Brother Petger." She began to cry and said, "I'll not go there!" I rejoiced over this decision. But now Katharina was called a second time to appear as a witness, but no one said a thing so I remained still, too. Then she was called for a third time. Then the judge asked another judge, the women judge, Kathajewa, "Isn't the father of Katharina here?" Now I made myself known. The judge asked, "Why is your daughter Katharina not present here?" I answered, "I showed her the summons, but she said, "I'm not going there, so she went to play with the children." The judge demanded of me, "Go at once and fetch your daughter here."

But I replied then, "Katharina has been interrogated in school without the knowledge of her parents. That is against the law of this land. Neverthe-less she was interrogated as though she were an adult. So let her now decide for herself whether she will come or not, but I cannot fetch her." Then the judge was angered and he slapped a fine on me, "That'll cost you fifty rubles!" Then one witness after another was called up-they were all unbelievers — and interrogated. They made Peter Petger appear as though he held worship services without permission, and had built a tabernacle for our gatherings. Most of all they portrayed him as one who religiously sought to influence children and youth. But no one could bring real wrong doing against him. To the contrary it was revealed that Peter Petger was an upright and dependable man. The assistant of Peter Petger, H. E., did say that he had not wanted to let children come to the worship service, because one could also train them as Christians at home. Thereupon, screamed the judge at Peter Petger, "Why have you not listened to your Brother? He has warned you, and in spite of it you did what you did!"

Peter Petger answered nothing. He remained still and calm throughout the entire case and said no unnecessary word, only replying when he had to. Completely alone he sat with shorn head on the bench of the accused. Each prisoner has his hair shorn. Only when his time of punishment is at an end dare he let his hair grow once again, usually during the last three months.

After the parade of witnesses, the state's attorney summed up the case naming Peter Petger as a criminal who had tried to corrupt children and young people. The full punishment of paragraph 136, namely five years in a concentration camp, should now be applied to him. The defense attorney, who according to the law should have defended Peter Petger, also declared him guilty instead of trying to help him. Only at the end of his speech did he mention that the court should keep it in mind that the accused had four innocent children at home and up to this time had never before sat on the bench of the accused. Perhaps he did not think about the consequence of what he had done. Brother Peter Petger himself declared in his last statement: "I am not guilty, I have followed the law of the state. But when any law is against the law of God I cannot follow it.

Thereupon the court adjourned to deliberate on the sentence. After two hours the sentence was announced: "Five years in a concentration camp!" Then the judge added to that the following words: "Abram Hamm will be punished with a fine of 50 rubles because he has refused to fetch his daughter Katharina as a witness to the court.

To conclude all the proceedings the judge announced that G. Klassen and I should be given over to the people's court. And this court should see to it that we should be arrested.

Chapter 9

Sowing Seed From God's Word In Jail

After our elder, Peter Petger, in the autumn of 1966, had been condemned to five years in concentration camp, we Brethren were called over and over again for hearings and threatened. Since it seemed to be a forgone conclusion that they were ready to condemn us too, my wife and I considered changing our residence, thinking of the words of Jesus: "If they persecute you in one town, then flee to another" (Matt 10:20). In January of 1967, I went to the Caucausus and visited several congregations there without having any clear leading whether we should move there. I stayed overnight with the elder of the congregation, Rudolf Klassen in Tbiliskaja, and there made the decision to travel next to Orenburg.

In the railroad station I had several hours of time to wait on the arrival of the train. Since I was somewhat chilled, I sat in the waiting room with my back to the oven, which helped to warm me up. Unfortunately, this did not last long for the militia officials appeared. One of them asked me, "What are you doing here?" "I want to travel to Orenburg to visit my mother. The train will not arrive for some time, and since I was chilled I wanted to warm myself beside this heater." Then came further questions. "Who are you? From where do you come? What do you want to do?" They demanded to see my pass, but I had only the drivers license for my motorbike. So the command rang out, "Come with us!" I was taken to the militia office. There these police searched my suitcase and found ten rubles under my soap. When they discovered this, I saw the money for the first time myself! "Why do you have this money hidden here?" "I did not put it there," said I. "Who then?" "I don't really know." Then it occurred to me that while I was staying in the Klassen home they could have put it

154

there. I told the police that it is a custom of believers to make a secret gift of money to their visitors, without saying anything about it to them. But the police did not believe this. Noticing that I had a German Bible as well as a Russian Bible in my suitcase they questioned me about them, especially about the German one. They said, "What is this?" "A German Bible," said I. "Ah ha, you want to preach here. That's what your Bibles demonstrate. Well, we're going to put a block in the way of that! We'll lock you up!" So I learned for the first time what the inside of the jail was like for ten days. My cell had only a small window, a wooden bench and in the corner a bucket for a toilet. That was the only furniture. A small glimmering light illuminated the cell somewhat; and with me in the cell were two younger and two older men.

"What law have you broken?" One of the older prisoners asked me. "None at all I answered. "That can't be. You must have done something!" he said. Upon this I told them what had happened to me. In conclusion I testified to them of my belief in Jesus Christ. Since it was already late in the evening I knelt down and prayed aloud. Then I wanted to lay down on the bench, but the two young men would not allow me to rest and stormed at me with many questions. Then the older ones said, "Now that is enough! Tomorrow you will still have plenty of time!" The thought went through my head, "Is this the place where I was going to live? Does my wife even suspect where I am locked up as a prisoner among other prisoners?"

Daily I was questioned by my fellow prisoners; by which they seemed to want to demonstrate to me that there could not be any God, or if there were he must be a stupid God.

On the next day we argued further. The oldest prisoner sat in a corner. Under his long black eyebrows he stared at me and said, "Abram is telling you fairy tales and old wives fables! Don't believe that nonsense!" Then I turned to him and said, "If you do not believe, you do not have to. But do you really want to be eternally lost?" "What?" said he, "Nobody has ever yet come back from life beyond! Who could even imagine that there could be some kind of life after death?" I answered, "Dear Sir, you say, 'There is no God,' but I am convinced that there is a God. Just suppose that you are right, and we both died. What would I have lost if there is no God?" He remained very still. And after a short time I said to him, "It would not have hurt me in any way. I would have tried to live a reasonable life, to be upright and honest, to have a successful marriage and to do good to other people. You would perhaps say that I could instead have done all the wicked things that I would have wanted to. That's true too, that I could have done that, but what would it have gained me? And furthermore, if there is a God, what have I lost?" He remained quiet and thoughtful. "Now I am going to tell you about that. You have lost eternal life. Not for a hundred or a thousand or a million years, but eternally, that means it never comes to an end! Is that correct?"

"Naturally that is correct if there is a God," he said, "but there is none!"

On the next to the last day he came to me, reached his hand under his jacket laying it upon his heart and said, "Do you know, here on my heart lies a hard and heavy stone. If I could only get rid of that I would do everything! Even if I would have to crawl on my knees and elbows to the most distant city." "My dear sir, you don't have to go on all fours creeping to the farthest city. Here in this very cell, and in this moment you can get rid of that burden. We can kneel down and ask the Lord Jesus for forgiveness. Then you will be free of your heavy stone. Are you ready to try that?" "Ah that is too simple!" "Yes, it is simple. We are not lost because of our sins, but because we have not believed in Jesus who has taken our sins upon himself upon the cross!" He could not conceive of it. Whether he did do it later I do not know; I've never seen him again. Oftentimes I sang beautiful songs of faith. The youngest of the prisoners was very inspired by the songs. He wrote them down and would have gladly learned to sing them. "I would really like to teach them to you, but here we are not alone!" Then he said, "Then we can do this very softly over there in the corner." So it came about that in the corner we practiced these songs very softly until he could sing them right.

On the eleventh morning the knocker on our cell door sounded. The trap door was opened and my name was called. "Get ready with your things!" A few minutes later I heard the ringing and jingling of the big bundle of keys and the door opened. I was fetched to the office of the director of the jail. He held my Russian Bible in his hand and asked me many questions about my faith. With a cheerful heart I could testify to him that I believe in the living God and that Jesus Christ is my Savior, that the Lord had done very many wonderful things for myself and my wife. This interview lasted an entire hour and than I could go. I was free! With thanks to God I still look back on these ten days in jail as an opportunity where I could sow the seeds of God's Word. God himself can rule and overrule so that the seed sown can bring forth fruit.

Chapter 10

Arrested For Investigation

In the spring of 1967, I was frequently called to hearings. **Always** the charge was that we were holding worship services, especially with children and youth, and we should cease to do so. We were summoned so many times to these hearings that they no longer bothered me. My wife noticed this and said, "It seems to me, as though you are not even worried about these summons anymore."

The growing crowded condition of our little group for their worship services, held here and there in private houses — also by us — brought me to the following thought. "What if I took this part of our house which up to now housed the cow and my motorcycle, broke out some walls, and then made it into a larger room in which our whole congregation could regularly assemble. I told my wife nothing of my thoughts for a long time, for I frequently felt that she was not ready for such a step. When I finally shared this plan with her she said, "That will not turn out well!" But I could not forget this idea. Always and again I went through these three little rooms, measured them with my ruler, and rejoiced to think about changing them. One day I started to break out the first wall. My wife hurried over and asked, "What are you doing there?" I answered, "What I told you about; that is what I am now beginning to do!" She said nothing further and went into the kitchen. After a time I looked into the kitchen at her. There she stood at the table and the tears ran down over her cheeks. "Why do you weep?" She answered, "They have called you so many times to a hearing and warned you that we could not even have worship services anymore in private houses. And now you want to make a larger worship service in our own house. They are going to lock us up soon." This stood like a dark cloud over my wife.

But after a time with God's help she overcame her fear and said, "Your decision was correct!" Even later after my arrest she stood true to her conviction on this matter and kept our house regularly open for worship services. Even though she was summoned to a hearing and fined with a money fine, she did not allow herself to be frightened. How this caused me to rejoice and strengthened me in the concentration camp when I heard about it!

Some men in our congregation helped in the remodeling of this assembly room. After everything was ready we invited the congregation in and everyone rejoiced. (When we were able to emigrate later in 1970, we made a present of this assembly room which comprised a third of our house. The rest of our house we sold for as much money as we needed to buy tickets for our travel out of the country. The congregation gave the whole house over to a believing young married couple to live in because it could not be listed as a meeting house alone. To this day worship services of our congregation take place there, even though the authorities keep threatening confiscation of it).

I, myself could only enjoy two worship services there. On the 6th of May I was summoned again to a hearing. The state prosecutor said, "Now the cup is full! Take your ball point pen and write: 'I Abram Hamm have made myself responsible to promise never again to permit youth to attend worship services. I myself will stand at the entrance of the meeting room and turn away all persons under 18 years of age.' " But such a promise I could not give. It was against God's will and my conscience. For this reason I declared, "I cannot do it! I rejoice when children and youth come to the services. We forced nobody to visit our congregation, we only invite; but we exclude nobody unless one would behave in a disorderly manner and disturb the service. With us any and all are welcome, old and young, big and little, poor and rich, Germans and Russians, Kirgisian and Ukrainian. We rejoice over each one who comes to us and we rejoice doubly when anyone is converted to God."

After this speech the official said, "Follow me!" I thought, "Now everything is at an end; I will never come home again!" He led me to the chief prosecutor and said, "Take a look at this man! He will not give in for anything and he promises nothing." Once again there was a long discussion. In conclusion I said, "And if I would be threatened by Breshnev himself, I would not say anything else except, 'I cannot do it.' " "Then we are going to put you in jail," was his answer. Thereupon I could only say, "That's up to you, but I will not do what I cannot do!" Then the officials were tired of so much speaking and said, "Get out! Go Home!" How glad I was that I had not done anything against God's Word, and in spite of it, I was allowed to go home again!

It was already very late. The last bus that I could take would not go all the way to our village and I still had to go five kilometers on foot. I lifted up my hand and waved. Suddenly the truck stopped and out of the seemingly full cabin came a voice, "Climb in!" I said, "But you don't have anymore room. Then the ones inside shouted, "Yes there is more room! It is a little narrow but not too bad!" So I climbed in. It smelled of whiskey, for the whole crew, including the driver, were drunk. They were howling songs to one another, and the driver was going in curvy snake lines. Left and right on either side of the road were deep ditches. Fortunately, there was no traffic. I prayed, "Lord, let me live through this experience!" These five kilometers seemed endless to me. But suddenly we came to our village and quickly I climbed out. My wife had been waiting for a long time and thought, "Will he be able to come back this time?" But now I was there and could tell her how it had gone in the hearing and then in the truck afterwards. We were full of thanks for God's gracious protection. Four days later on the 10th of May, 1967, the militia police drove up to our house and demanded us to come with them. Up to now I was always summoned in writing, but this time the militia police themselves came; that made me think. So I spoke up and said, "I'll come tomorrow because it is already evening and the workday is over." But they answered, "If you don't come of your own free will we will use force on you!" I saw of course that resistance would be in vain and drove with them to Tokmak. At the police station I was led into an empty room and there I had to empty all of my pockets and take off my belt. All of my buttons were examined and those that were made of metal were cut off. I even had to take off most of my clothing so that it could be examined in detail and then I could get dressed again.

Now I knew the time is here. During the past 19 years the Lord has prepared me for this time! That made me feel at peace for I knew that I would be hidden in my Lord's hands. Then a militia police officer led me through a long hallway. On both sides I saw doors that were locked with big locks. In front of one door the officer stood, opened it up and said, "Go inside!" I stepped in and the door slammed shut behind me. In the cell there was only a small bulb burning. In this room there stood a wooden bench and a toilet in the corner. That was all. Four men looked curiously at me. There was still room on the bench. I was glad for that because otherwise I would have to sleep on the cold cement floor and use only the clothing I had with me as mattress, cover and pillow.

The four prisoners besieged me with questions. "What have you done?" "Nothing," said I. "Now stop that! They don't put you in this lock up just for nothing." One said, "We were all put in here for nothing." I said, "I believe in Jesus Christ. I have permitted children and young people to come to the worship service and told them about the living God." Then they really became excited and questioned me further. The questioning lasted until late in the night. They had hardly heard anything about God and Jesus. Then one said to me, "Are you also able to pray?" I said, "If you are still, so that I can concentrate then I will also pray. I knelt down and prayed half aloud and nobody bothered me.

After a few days I was fetched out of the cell, taken to the railroad station and transported to Frunza, the capital city of Kirgisian. There in the main prison I was taken with other prisoners to the bath. Our hair was shorn off completely and our clothing was deloused. After that they locked us up again in cells. I was never in one cell for very long. I accepted that God directed it this way so that I could witness for Jesus Christ. Once a day the guards led us into an exercise room. The high walls were without a window. And above us instead of a ceiling and a roof there was only barbed wire so that we would be able to see the light coming in. On a gallery watching over us stood guards with weapons. We were not permitted to work in jail and the food was miserable. Food was shoved in to us through a small opening in the cell door. It was too little to live, and to much to die.

Then I knew that because of my testimony for Jesus I would be robbed of my freedom. And this made me able to bear the misery of imprisonment better, than that of the other prisoners. God also granted me that, despite all the difficulties, I could remain completely calm even during the hearings. I sat once for several hours before the investigative judge, Krudajberdejew. He examined me concerning my faith and said, "Now I know everything about you. I know, too, that your children are better than ours." I asked, "What do we actually do that is evil enough to have us arrested? We teach and train our children that they should obey the laws of the state, do their duty, and live a decent life. And they do those things!" During this conversation I noticed that his eyes became moist. He answered, "I know that what you are saying is right! But our system wants to exterminate all religion. And we cannot change that. You will have to be condemned!" I understood that he would lose his job if he would let me go; even if he did not give expression to this thought.

How important it is to receive letters, never became so apparent to me until after my arrest and imprisonment. Before that I had never enjoyed writing letters; I left that to my wife. In prison we could neither write letters nor receive them. Only when we were in the concentration camp was that allowed. But sometimes it would happen that one would be in jail for several months, and some for an entire year before one would be sent to the concentration camp. In spite of this I tried everything I could to get news to my relatives outside the prison. Sometimes when a prisoner would be released I would send a letter along with him written on the thick paper of cement sacks. In this way my wife received news from me several times. But she still could not send me any letters. Then suddenly she thought of a beautiful thing. She would write a letter, get ready a cloth bag and hide this inside a loaf of bread and bake it. Then she would go on the bus to Tokmak, deliver this package to the guards, and a short time later I would have it in my cell. This happened just 10 minutes before my transportation to the main prison in Frunza. I rejoiced over the beautiful fresh bread, conscious of the proverb which says, "The way to a man's heart is through his stomach. I divided the bread with the four other prisoners in our cell. I knew nothing of this letter from my wife. And I did not even find it in the loaf.

In the main prison of Frunza we five prisoners never came together again in one cell. However, later in the concentration camp I did meet one of them again. Then one of them told me, "As I bit into my piece of bread at that time, I noticed that paper was in it. Cautiously I took it out and thought, this has got to be a letter. But I could not read it for the script was unknown to me. That was probably German. I have looked everywhere to find you. I even called into other cells through the window, asking, 'Is Abram Hamm among you?' But everything was in vain. Then there came an intensive search, and they took this letter away from me."

One day we prisoners at Frunza were loaded up and transported to Tokmak which is 60 kilometers away. One after another was called up and had to go into the, so called, black punishment wagon used to transport prisoners. The few seats were soon occupied and we called, "The car is full!" But the officers pushed in more prisoners. I was pushed in, too, even though there was not enough space for me. I was actually squeezed in so that only one foot was on the floor. Once I tried to put my foot down on the floor. This way it would rest the other foot. This I was unable to do because the space was already occupied by someone else's foot. Now I could not touch the floor anymore and the whole weight of my body pressed against another prisoner. We were wedged in so thickly on top of one another that nobody knew who was laying on whom. With force I tried to at least put one foot on the floor once again. I shoved and pushed and begged those near me to give a little bit, and finally I succeeded in touching the floor with one foot.

The sun burned strongly on the roof of the truck and besides that, many of the prisoners were smoking. The air was now unbearably hot and polluted with tobacco smoke. As a non-smoker I found this especially nauseating. It seemed to me as though I would choke. I wanted to scream out, "Just stop smoking a little bit!" But I knew that it would be useless to try to tell them something like that. For this reason I sighed deeply in my heart to God, "Lord! help me! What's going to happen to me here!" Hardly had I prayed with myself in this manner, than there came a big loud voice out of one corner, "Stop smoking! Do you think we want to be suffocated?" This came from one known as a most dangerous bandit. From then on nobody smoked. They all obeyed the bandit. And how I thanked my God for this quick answer to prayer!

It still was a long time before the smoke disappeared because the small window was locked. This tortuous trip lasted two hours until the truck reached the courtyard of the prison in Tokmak.

We were all drenched with sweat. It was as if we had just come from the water and our limbs pained us. But even so there was still a wait until we could leave our sweatbox. When the door was opened we poured out of the truck. Some of the prisoners screamed, "Do you want to murder us, or what are you thinking of doing? How come you crammed the truck so full that we couldn't even put our feet on the floor? And that was done in this heat!" The answer came back loud and clear, "We didn't invite you here! If you hadn't done something stupid you would all still be in freedom."

Chapter 11

As Accused Before The Court In Tokmak

In the middle of 1967, my court process in Tokmak took place. As I was fetched out of my cell, my fellow prisoners asked me, "How long do you suppose you will get?" I lifted my hand showing five fingers and said, "I imagine 5 years imprisonment." I knew that Peter Petger had also received five years in the concentration camp.

The militia led me into the courtroom and then allowed me to greet my relatives. My 78 year old mother, and my sisters Anna and Elizabeth who had come from Orenburg on the long journey began to cry. I said to them, "Here we do not cry! That we do at another place and for something else!" With my wife I had already made promise that we would not cry — conscious of the words: "Show me not your sorrow before the false world."

The courtroom was not very large. Consequently all of the believers who had come, could not get in. My wife and seven children sat behind me on the wooden bench. I sat on the accused bench. The female judge glanced at my wife and children and seemed to have some sympathy because she noticed that my wife was expecting a child (one month later on the 15th of August this child was born; a boy named Heinrich). Nine months earlier the judge had sentenced Peter Petger to five years in the concentration camp; and later had said to his wife, "After the sentencing I was unable to sleep for the whole night because the sentence was too harsh. Now perhaps she was thinking of that, for her eyes glanced at my wife and me, looking at us with a very mild expression.

Before the judge officially opened the case, she gave the summary of the regulations of the court and asked me if I had any objections; and if I would allow myself to be represented by a defense attorney. I replied,

"No, I renounce a defense attorney." This was namely because I thought, "How could an atheist put in a good word for me?" And even if he would have dared, he would bring himself in danger! That I did not want. Thereupon the judge asked, "Do you want to defend yourself?" I answered, "I have a Defender", and I pointed with my hand to heaven. After this I had to put my signature to a statement that I had renounced a defense attorney, and consequently he left the room. The judge now declared, "With us in the Soviet Union nobody is punished because of his belief. But believers are not permitted by law to make religious propaganda nor to influence other people religiously. Above all they may not train children religiously. They have the duty to train up their children in the communist ideology, that means atheistically."

She then asked me what my opinions were on the registrations of congregations. I answered, "I would be for it, if we were today to be registered. That startled her into saying "How, citizen accused? What do you mean by that?" Probably she thought that during my imprisonment I had come to some accommodating insight. I replied, "Just as I said. I am not opposed to the registration of the congregation itself, because according to the law, state and church should be separated. The church is, as a matter of fact, separated from the state. But the whole thing is crooked. Is the state actually separated from the church? Or does it not make (with its many regulations and restrictions on the church) the case to be that it is dictating and restricting the church. This should not be that the state mixes itself into questions of faith and belief; but rather as it was in the beginning of this century in the Soviet Union. Then the state did not mix itself in with the matters of faith." After this statement the witnesses were called and testified that I was a leader in the congregation and that I was in charge of pushing children and youth work. Some of them didn't know me at all and had never been present in a worship service; for example two teachers.

One of these women teachers was asked, "Do you know the accused Abram Hamm? And what can you testify of him?" She answered, "Personally, I do not know him. My students have told me that he is the organizer of the congregation." The other woman teacher declared, "My own children play with the neighbor's children." They heard them say, "Uncle Hamm leads the congregation." An old man by the name of Tkatschow testified, "I have spoken with Abram Hamm and declared to him, 'That's all nonsense what you believe. When I was young I belonged to the Orthodox faith and was very pious. But I have long since seen that there is no

God; and if you train up children to believe that there is, you make them spiritual cripples.' " Another witness said, "I was already with them in the worship service. There he had preached, children said poems and young people sang and prayed. Then I noticed how backward these youth were. People like Abram Hamm are responsible for this. They are making the youth stupid. The state should move sharply against them.

After the witness had their say, time was given me to testify. Turning to the female judge I said, "I know that you are going to condemn me, but I don't know on what ground and on which testimony you will be able to do this, unless it would be on what children have said in the school yard or in the street. I have not done anything worthy of punishment. We live according to the constitution in a so-called land of religious freedom. In school we had sung the song, "I know of no other land where one can breathe so free!" But now, however, I'm sitting on the accused bench and I am going to be judged." Then began the midday pause. All spectators had to leave the room, only my relatives dare remain. The militia police who was guarding me did not lead me back to the cell; but allowed me to stay with my relatives. In order to do this, he had to miss his lunch and stay in the room with me. God had given him the strength to do this. I could meanwhile eat of the bread that had been brought along, and visit with my wife and children. Walter Wadel and Gustav Fenskij from Jurjewka, as well some other Brethren from our congregation, came to the window and spoke to me encouraging me that I should not do anything foolish; and that I should not do anything against God's Word.

After the one-hour recess the trial was continued. I was astonished when the state prosecutor demanded only three years in concentration camp, because I had counted on getting five years. Even more astonishing was the judgment that was finally handed down. How I thanked my Redeemer, Jesus Christ, that he had softened the heart of my judge so much that she gave me this mild judgment, — mild for soviet standards. I was also glad that I did not have to beg the court for mercy. Then I could see how the Lord himself had interceded for me. I was especially thankful that I had not said anything against God's Word and had not wounded my conscience. I had only the protective mercy of my Lord to thank for that.

After the case was concluded I was led, by a soldier with weapons, on foot to the 500 meter punishment cell. My wife and some Brethren accompanied me. A young man went very closely behind me, and as the guard looked to one side, he stuck something into my pocket. Coming to the cell I looked and found six rubles. I gave the guard two rubles, because he missed his lunch for my sake. I later learned to know the young man who had given me the six rubles, sticking them into my pocket. He was Johann Kinas, a true Christian from the Pokrowka congregation in the vicinity of Tokmak. Later, he himself was arrested and condemned to five years in the concentration camp.

My fellow prisoners in the cell naturally asked me immediately, "How many years have they given you?" They rejoiced sincerely that I only had been given a year and six months, "Actually, they should have let you go free because you really didn't do anything against the law," was their opinion. Not always did prisoners speak so well of the believers. Often the saying was, "They should hang you up from the telephone poles."

When peace reigned once more in the cell, I threw myself in the corner with my face on the bench. I felt guilty about it that I was so mildly punished while Peter Petger was given five years. Had I perhaps said something which was against God's Word? But on reflecting over everything, I could find nothing wrong with what was said. For this reason I began to give thanks and prayed, "Lord Jesus, you were by me, and you have directed and cared for everything so that I was not punished cruelly. It is your goodness and grace, and I thank you!"

It was clear to me that I would be transported away in a short time. Friends of mine had heard about this and begged for permission to visit me a little yet. One day the clapper in our cell door opened and an officer called, "Hamm, get yourself ready to say some good-byes!" Shortly after that, he opened the door and led me through the long passageway through the corridor. There awaited some Brethren for me from the Pokrowka congregation. Peter Klassen I knew already, and the other two who were Willie Nikel and Franz Kröker, I learned to know. The last one named, knew one of the officers and had worked out permission for this meeting with him. Otherwise it was almost impossible for even next of kin to meet with a condemned prisoner before his transport even for only five minutes. But here were new acquaintances that had been permitted to come. This was very extraordinary! Through these Brethren I was consoled and strengthened and was very thankful for the visit. One of them stuck something in my pocket; later I found it to be ten rubles. Now I possessed altogether 14 rubles. In the prison camp these were taken from me but written down on a list as my property. From this money I would be able to buy some bread from time to time.

My wife had asked the judge for permission to see me a little bit before I was transported. And that was permitted. She could bring me clean clothes and speak with me for five minutes; also my oldest daughter, Maria, was there. We did not dare to speak German with one another; only Russian, so that the guards could understand everything.

Two days later my transportation to the prison in Frunza began. My wife had found out when the train would travel through our station of Iwanowka. She stood with our children and the whole congregation beside the track at the railroad station. I greeted all of them through the window with a few words; but then the watching soldier shut the window so that I could not say anymore. The youth group of our congregation sang songs of faith and accompanied it with music. The people outside held my children up to the window one after another so that I could see them once more. One of the believing Brethren quoted loudly, so I could hear, from Psalm 37:37; Notice the upright man, his end shall be peace. I could still hear it well, and then the train began to move once again. The youth sang and played wholeheartedly. The whole congregation walked along beside the train and sang and waved. Thus, I had a foretaste of heaven, even though a hard time awaited me in concentration camp. My fellow prisoners and the soldiers of the watch were astonished and asked me, "To whom do all of these people and youth belong?" Then I had the opportunity to tell that we all belonged to Jesus Christ. As Brethren and Sisters we belonged together, and in spite of all oppression and difficulty we are consoled because we see God's caring hand held over us.

Chapter 12

In The Camp At Kirowka

On a beautiful summer day the beginning of August, 1967, I and thirty five other prisoners were taken from the jail in Frunza to the railroad station. Each had received a piece of bread in his hand. "Water you will receive on the train"—so we were told. Soldiers with guns and fierce dogs accompanied us to the train wagons.

We were not told the goal of this journey, but we knew that about 400 kilometers away, the concentration camp of Kirowka was situated. In the train cars it was very warm because it was jammed full of people. The soldiers of the guard, locked the door from the outside so that no one could escape. During the journey we received water to drink. At the railroad station of Dshambul we were allowed to leave the car. Weaponed soldiers with fierce dogs took charge of us, and led us to the ready trucks. We then traveled about 60 kilometers to the camp. The officials of the camp looked closely at each prisoner and saw what his crime was according to his papers. As the chief of the camp looked at my papers he said, "What, only a year and six months? You should have gotten ten years!" Without thinking further I replied, "And if they would have given me fifty years that would have changed nothing."

The camp barracks were overfilled and there was no more room for us. We had to remain outside and first build a kind of rough pavilion and then throw up bunks two beds high in it. Forty of us were housed in that structure. During the summer one could do rather well, but in winter when the temperature outside fell to 30 below zero it was terribly cold in our shed. To be sure an iron stove stood in it. But it was only heated up sometimes. Most of the time we received neither wood nor coal for heating. Each of us 40 prisoners tried to bring little pieces of wood back from the work area, hiding them. But often these were discovered by the controllers and taken away.

From the first day on I kept asking my fellow prisoners if there were any other believers in the concentration camp. I was pointed to one man, went up to him and asked, "Are you a believer?" He said, "That, I am not!" And so it went with me when I asked the second and the third. These were decent people, but did not know anything of Jesus Christ. The opinion in the camp was, if anyone doesn't curse nor drink and remains a decent person, he is probably a believer. But that does not always work that way. For a whole week long I sought in vain and felt rather forsaken. In prayer I asked the Lord, "What shall I do here?" Then came the answer in my mind that Jesus had told his disciples, "You will be my witnesses." (Acts 1:8). That was for me a confirmation. Here my task is to tell the prisoners about Jesus. This was not easy, for many of them were atheistically trained and had a criminal mentality besides. Unfortunately, I had no Bible, not even a New Testament; only Bible verses which I had earlier learned by memory stood ready for my use. They were a tremendous treasure to me. I decided at that point that whenever I would have a chance in the future I would learn many more Bible verses by memory.

Only thirty five kilometers away from our camp, in Leninpol, my brother Jacob lived. One of our overseers was a Muslim Kirgise and came out of the same village. My brother had worked for him earlier and befriended him. One day this overseer told me that he had been by my brother and he had asked him if he could send me some food and a little book. He declared that he was ready to do that, even though he was appointed to watch over me and guard me. Immediately it came to my mind, that little book is a New Testament. I could have jumped high for joy. But it turned out other than I expected. On the next day I was called and told that there was a visitor for me. I thought that'll be my brother Jacob; for my wife could not come since she was expecting a child. Near by the concentration camp gate stood a building in which the prisoners could meet with their relatives. As a matter of fact I met my brother Jacob there. He had brought a bundle of food with him that probably weighed about 10 kilograms. Only 5 kilograms were allowed. The guard who had to search through all the things that were brought by relatives saw this bundle but did not weigh it and only said, "Well, I suppose that's about 5 kilos in weight." With one voice we both answered, "Yes, there are probably that many kilos in there!" Since it was warm summer weather, we were permitted to sit outside in the courtyard and visit for two hours. A guard always went up and down to observe us. I noticed that my brother was somewhat excited. As soon as the guard had turned his back my brother took something out of his boot and stuck it into mine. I knew what that was, namely the New Testament; and rejoiced inwardly. We entertained one another for a while longer and let on as though nothing had happened. After the visit of my brother I prayed, "Lord, help me, that this New Testament would not be found." And it turned out that I was not searched. How God can lead, ruling and overruling among men! I was very cheerful and hurried to my place in the camp. To me it was as though someone had given me a jewel, or a great piece of gold, as it says in Psalm 119:162, I rejoice over thy Word like a man that has found treasure.

I often had to hide my New Testament and was thankful that it was such a small size. Sometimes I put it underground, other times between boards, between other books, and old clothes. I have carried it under my shirt and stuck it into my boots. Finally I found a very secure hiding place. I made a deeper cut in a very thick board and the little book went right in this space. It was never found in any search, and so through God's goodness I was able to keep it until my eventual release from prison.

Once in our concentration camp it was announced that anybody who could understand glass-cutting should report to the authorities. I reported myself, and was forwarded to another work brigade which was building a house about 8 kilometers distant from the camp. It was winter and icy cold. We prisoners always had to sit on the open truck in rows of five. Until we had finally been counted and released for work, we had to keep on sitting there until we were thoroughly chilled and our teeth chattered. Most of us wore only thin shoes or old boots, and as a result our feet became icy cold. For this reason we prisoners jumped up and down and back and forth on the truck. This caused the vehicle to shake around so much that the driver couldn't drive very well. When we arrived at the building site which was surrounded by barbed wire, it seemed to take endlessly long until the guard had taken the roll call and put us to work. We could not even get off the truck without these formalities.

Going on to the construction site, I measured the windows and cut the window glass to fit. A helper brought the window panes to the window frames and fastened them with small nails. In my workroom I had a small iron oven burning; for with completely cold and clammy hands, I would be unable to cut the glass properly. This oven was also precious to us because we could bake potatoes in it. In the concentration camp we received very few potatoes, but the truck driver, Theodor Giesbrecht from Lenin pol, who had to bring much construction material to this construction site, did not mind bringing some potatoes from his family, or from my brother Jacob, or from the little congregation in Leninpol.

The elder of this little congregation, Heinrich Löwen, wanted to visit me once. Really this was only permitted to near relatives, but we had begged the soldiers on watch to permit Brother Löwen to come to this construction site so that he could speak with me. One day I was summoned, "There is a visitor for you there." There stood a big, stately man before me and greeted me heartily. The soldier allowed us to have a few hours together in my warm work room. During this time I did not need to work. We prayed with one another, then Brother Löwen reached down and handed to me a big package of foods. He also asked how things were going for us prisoners. In this way he found out that our feet were miserably freezing because we had such poor footwear. Then he said at once, "Take off your boots!" And at the same time he took off his. "So, now try these boots of mine on!" I slipped into them. They were wonderfully warm because they were still new, and they were well insulated and they fit me. Then he said, "Now we have exchanged boots. Mine are yours now, and yours are mine! I could hardly grasp this because my own boots were already old and thin. What I felt can only be understood by someone who has had to work continually in the open air at -20 to -30 below zero! I could only thank the Brother with a few inadequate words. Also, I thanked the Lord Jesus for this from the bottom of my heart that he had made a Brother who was hitherto unknown to me so warm hearted in helping. Yes, here a warm heart had brought warm boots!

On the 7th of November, 1967, was the fiftieth anniversary of the Russian Revolution. Already from the first day of our being in a concentration camp, prisoners were looking forward to this great event. They said, "Fifty years' anniversary of the soviet regime — there will certainly be a great amnesty and we will all be allowed to go home." This saying went like a forest fire through the whole camp. New rumors were always being spread, something that is a custom of prisoners, and various reports circulated. With this the prisoners consoled one another and encouraged one another.

When the 7th of November arrived, we were all sitting in our shed and listening to the radio news. A skilled technician among the prisoners had put together, and made workable a kind of radio. Finally the news began. In friendly tones, an exciting voice said, "Dear countrymen, our glorious country in the last fifty years has advanced greatly in technology and social life. Our regime is deeply filled with humanitarian interest. And for this reason it has prepared for this day a great amnesty for all prisoners who are confined. All those with a punishment time up to two years will be released to go home, as well as all those who are for the first time in prison. Punishment times over two years will be cut in half."

Hardly was this announcement made over the radio, when all the prisoners began to shout, "Amnesty! Amnesty! Amnesty! Tomorrow we are going home!" Even my heart wanted to jump for joy. I had received a year and a half of concentration camp confinement. And I also had been condemned for the first time. Surely I would be eligible for immediate release. The following night I will never forget. Nobody slept and all sat in groups together and spoke about it that at last they would be allowed to go home. They made tea and used up all the provisions which they had been saving up to moment.

Unfortunately, the way it was painted for us never came to pass. The release of prisoners from the amnesty was spread out over the next eight weeks. The officials had unfortunate experiences from the amnesty that followed Stalin's death in 1953. The prisoners were all released at one shot and crowded into the railroad stations, many becoming drunken, rioting, stealing the things for sale and beginning fights. With this there arose such battles many times with fatal outcomes. The police were now determined that such disorder would never happen again. Many landed right back in prison and thus their amnesty was wasted.

Day after day I waited in vain for my amnesty, and accompanied many released prisoners to the gate of the camp. Finally I could wait no longer, and reported to the camp authorities, asking them when it would be my turn. Then they told me brutally, "You are worse than a bandit!" I answered, "How so? What bad thing had I done?" "Yes, the bandit strikes another person dead, but you make many people to become mental cripples through your belief on Jesus. You are too dangerous! They should have condemned you to ten years of confinement!"

Already they had told me in an earlier hearing, "You Christians should be sent into perpetual exile where no other humans are, and only the polar bears live. There you could pray as long as you wanted." I remained completely calm at this. Then the KGB officer became furious and screamed, "You should be beaten until the feathers fly off you. Your name shouldn't be Hamm but Sham because you are an idiot and a vulgar person!"

So I learned that in the Soviet Union, a Christian is much too dangerous and is considered much more so than the worst criminal. Then I thought, the Lord Jesus has taken upon himself such bitter suffering for me, that I should also be ready to suffer for his name's sake.

My wife and children had also heard of the amnesty. They waited with great joy day after day for my return home. But they waited in vain. They had to learn that criminals and bandits will be released, but for Christians there is no amnesty. We consoled ourselves with the certainty that we as citizens of heaven have received an eternal amnesty from God for our sins and that no one can hold them against us anymore. I was not permitted to go home until the rest of my one and a half years had been fulfilled.

Chapter 13

Each Helps Carry The Other's Burden

After a few months Herman Wall was brought into the camp. He belonged to the registered church in Leninpol. As soon as I asked him whether he believed on Jesus Christ he confirmed it. From the heart I rejoiced for now I would not be the only believer here. After a short time Herman confessed to me, "I have been lukewarm and have become spiritually flack, but I would like to begin anew. That is no doubt why God has brought me into this camp. When you have the time I want to confess before you my sins. It stands written in 1 John 1:9, "If we confess our sins he is faithful and just to forgive us our sins and to cleanse us from all unrighteousness." Also it says in James 5:16, "Confess to one another your sins." So we covenanted to meet on the next rest day. This would have been the day after tomorrow. But already on the next day I felt myself pressed in the spirit to look up Herman and say to him, "If you want to speak out then be sure that you confess all your sins and do not remain silent about any of them. I say that, not because your sins interest me, but because that's the only way you will get peace and freedom if you confess them all. That I know from my own experience." He took my counsel thankfully and confessed that he had been planning to be silent about one matter because he was too ashamed about it.

We had a wonderful brotherly relationship after that, and promised to pray with each other every morning before work. But it was hard for him to get up earlier. To me it made no difference, because I longed for this quiet time when no other people were around to disturb. Always when I came to wake up my friend I saw that he was till in a deep sleep and out of pity I let him sleep until the general wake-up time. Until one day he said to me, "If only you would have awakened me, we would have been able to pray together for the hard day ahead of us!" From then on I did this. We shared everything together in prayer, even the smallest things. In his childhood Herman had learned Kirgisian and spoke it well. One day we were looking for a place to pray undisturbed. We had promised one another that if anyone would come up and see us praying the one who would not be praying should explain what we were doing. We went then to some bushes and knelt down together. While I prayed two observers from a distance cried out, "What are you doing there? Get up!" But I kept on praying and thought, Herman will certainly explain to the observers what we are doing. But he did not stand up and continued to pray, too. When we had ended I asked him, "Why didn't you stand up and go to the observers?" He answered, "Those were Kirgisian men. As they were still close I heard one of them say to the other, "They are praying! Let them be."

My time of punishment came to an end on the 10th of November, 1968. I was glad that I had suffered for the sake of Jesus and was not put into the concentration camp for some time. And Herman Wall rejoiced that his time in the camp had brought him to a revival. We both confessed that God makes no mistake even when he leads us on hard roads. Herman said, "I rejoice from my heart that you have come here." Thereupon I answered, "It makes me sad that you will have to remain here, four more years after I leave." On the last day Herman accompanied me to the camp door. There we took leave of one another, then the door shut behind me and I was free. How I felt can hardly be described! I went about 300 meters further and knelt down to thank my Lord that I could be free once again. Then I prayed for Herman and for all those in the camp to whom I had spoken about Jesus Christ.

Herman's own time in the camp was shortened. Afterwards he joined one of the unregistered congregations in Leninpol. Later, he was called to be deacon in that church. Since then many years have gone by, but the remembrance of our brotherly relationship has not dimmed; nor has it been forgotten, but has always been engraved in my heart.

That little group of believers in Leninpol who had been excluded from the Mennonite Brethren Church there, because they would not accept registration, had drawn closer together and supported several families of imprisoned Brethren with clothes and money. It was through my brother Jacob in Leninpol that they had also helped me and my family while I was in camp. We hardly knew one another, but the love that we had for our common Lord let us become true Brethren; who are inwardly bound together in the sense of Christ's commandment that each one help to carry the other's burden." (Gal 6:2) This was of great meaning, for in the Soviet Union, even though there is a government welfare program, it does not cover the suffering families whose breadwinners have been imprisoned because of their faith. Were it not that in the year 1964, the Council of Help for Prisoners had been founded, and had not some believers in the congregations burdened themselves for the families of those in prison; many of those families would have starved to death.

Chapter 14

The Lord Cares For His Own
Maria's Experiences

Just before his first arrest my husband worked together with me in the sugar beet fields of the collective farm. Since it was hard to fill the quota assigned to us, our two oldest children also helped along. One day at the beginning of May, 1967, two militia police came and fetched my husband away from the field. That time he did come back, but on the 10th of May, he was arrested and taken to jail. With seven children I remained behind. The eighth one was on the way. Three months later in August of 1967, he was born. From then until the following spring I could not do anymore work on the collective farm. How would I and the children be able to survive? But our God did not leave us in the lurch. He made people willing to help us. During this time I regularly received as much money from the believers as my husband had formerly earned. During the cold season of the year members of our congregation provided wood and coal for us. In the spring the youth group dug up the garden. The Brethren put new shingles on our house roof, since the old had become rotten through decay.

The communist officials were not pleased at all that the godly congregation still met in our house. Over and over the KGB officials came, or the teacher, in order to search us. They wanted to force me to sign some kind of a paper but I refused to sign. Because as it often happened that someone who had signed one of their papers, had signed to untrue conclusions hidden in the wording.

In school our children had to suffer many disadvantages. They got bad reports even on their behavior. The teachers urged other children to attack them. Hardly a day went by in which they were not mocked or beaten by their fellow students. Because of this they were, of course, very with-drawn and often wept bitterly.

One day in November, 1967, my children said to me in a very excited way "Mama, a little bus has stopped outside. Who do they want to take away now?" I thought "Yes, now what is going to happen?" A man and two women came to our house. My heart beat fast and seemed to be chok-ing me. They came in and greeted us in a friendly manner. Then the man asked, "How are you doing?" I answered, "We're getting along." "Do you have bread?" "Yes, some." "Do you have flour?" "Still a little." "How many children do you have?" "Eight." Three of them stood beside me, and two held on to my dress while the smallest of all I had in my arms. They all looked at this man with great fear. "Where is your hus-band working?" "He is not here. He is in prison." "Why?" "Because of his faith." "Oh no, nobody is arrested." "Neverthe-less, they took him away because of his religion," said I. "From what do you live then?" "My husband had earned some before he was arrested, and I worked up to July in the sugarbeet fields." So from that we still had some money." (I did not want the whole world to know that we were receiving support from believers). "Now then, perhaps we can help you. You do not need to be ashamed to tell us that you have nothing more." I answered, "As it happens we still have something." In saying this I thought to myself, you want to help us, indeed, something like that has never happened before. You would probably much rather take away from us the last that we have!

About ten days later they came again. They came up to us in a friendly manner and held a paper in front of my nose and said, "Sign this please." But I answered, "I cannot sign anything so quickly. First I have to know what it is." Then the officials said, "We were here not long ago, and then made a report about how things are going with you. We have told the chief of our administration about you. He doesn't want that you are lacking on anything. So he, himself has ordered what we are to bring to you: two hundred kilograms of wheat, thirty kilograms of sugar, twenty kilograms of pork, and fifteen kilograms of dried fruit. I began to tremble from as-tonishment, and I could not imagine how a thing like this could happen. I signed the receipt and wanted to find a few sacks to put the food into. But I found no sacks, since just a short time ago I had purchased pig feed and used them to store it. Then the man said, "Well, we could just pour the wheat right on the floor here. Then later you could find sacks to put it in." Sugar and fruit I was able to put into some containers. I gave hearty thanks, and then they left again. Hardly were they away when someone from our congregation came and stood there astonished to see this miracle. Together we thanked the Lord that he never forgets his own.

Another time a Brother from the Bergtal congregation came and brought a sack of wheat and a sack of flour in the sidecar of his motorcycle. He said, "The Lord has sent me." Then I was deeply moved.

Many Brethren and Sisters in the faith, German as well as Russian, stood by us in these difficult times. They brought us food and provisions. They consoled me with the Word of God and prayed with us. That was for me a special strengthening. So I experienced again and again that God has not forgotten me. For my husband, this was also a special consolation whenever he learned of these things through my letters. It was always the wish that I gave expression to in my prayer that the Lord would richly bless and repay these faithful helpers. For it was not possible for me to do so. It was not even very easy for me to keep on accepting gifts like these; and I had to keep reminding myself of the Word of God in Acts 20:35, "It is more blessed to give than to receive!"

On Christmas evening on the year of 1967, we had in our congregation as usual, a Christmas story. The children sang songs and recited their poems, and they they awaited with great expectation the sharing out of presents. A little sack was given with candy and cookies for each one. In the families, themselves, the Christmas custom was like this. Before he went to sleep, each child placed a bowl on the table. Later the parents would lay presents in these. The next morning the children found these there. To the Christmas and Easter celebrations we attached a special significance. The congregation's choir sang; or some of the singers went from house to house to sing carols outside the windows, where they were invited. As a sign that one wanted to hear the carols, the door would be left unlocked, and the dog would be put into the shed. Then the church choir or even single singers came and stood at which ever doors were unlocked, while the people inside stayed in bed. All of a sudden I heard soft steps as we lay in bed. The door was cautiously opened and I heard whispering and I waited for the songs to start and was about to wake the children so that they would be able to hear the beautiful songs. But it remained quiet and the steps went away. After a while I got up in order to see what was happening. Through the window I could see two people going away. Then I went into the room. A big sack stood in the middle and on the table there lay a package for each child with his name on it and a Christmas greeting. Besides this, there was a large container of honey. Tears came into my eyes. Gladly I would have looked into the sack to see its contents, but since I was alone I thought I had better wait until the next morning and share the discovery with the children. The rejoicing on the following morning was indescribably great. We found a bedcover, a mattress, a pair of shoes for each child, something for each one to wear, and a Sunday shirt for my husband. We rejoiced over such abundance! Then we held our morning devotions. We thanked the Lord for this great kindness and asked him to bless those who had helped us in our need. Later we learned that believers from four hundred kilometers away in Leninpol had sent these Christmas gifts to us.

During the time that my husband was under arrest, I also received packets from foreign countries such as Austria, Switzerland, Sweden, Luxemburg, Holland, East Germany, West Germany, the United States and Canada. Where did the senders ever get our address?

Once a letter came with a square of chocolate in it. Another time one came with a tiny packet of powder to make a pudding accompanied by a card with Bible verses. Also some packages came with clothing. We were able to sell some of the things that came this way: and from the money, buy feed for the cow and the little pig. Otherwise we would not have been able to keep these animals.

Later after my husband had been released, a notice came to us that in a post office 25 kilometers away, a package from a foreign country had arrived for us. We went there and the post office official handed it to us. In this package which arrived we found five large tablecloths which were in size 1 1/4 meters by 1 1/4 meters; three of them were decorated with beautiful stripes. We had no idea what these tablecloths were worth. An acquaintance told us, "Such a thing is worth about 120 rubles in the market. I have seen such a cloth being sold for even as high as 150 rubles." We had no idea that such things would be sold at such prices. We did not want to make big profit. But even so, for three of the tablecloths we received 120 rubles, 80 rubles, and 70 rubles. And with the money we received from the sales of these three tablecloths we were able to buy another cow since the old one was sick and had to be slaughtered.

We could only pray in astonishment at how the Lord had made people willing to help us. Even the knowledge that believers even those from the other side of the globe — were thinking of us in prayer and by gifts, strengthened us in our faith. We knew that we were not forgotten.

Chapter 15

Who Is Ruining The Children

Because of the worship services that were held in our house, I was fined by the officials more than once. At first it was twenty rubles, then fifty and finally sixty. From the 12 rubles of child support which I received monthly since I could not work, they could not subtract anything. And since I could not pay the money fined, I was summoned before the court. My husband, who meanwhile had been released, came along as a translator because I could speak Russian only very poorly. The female judge asked my husband, "What do you want here, you haven't been summoned!" He answered, "My wife speaks Russian only very poorly." For this reason she allowed him to come into the room. Then the woman judge asked me, "Why have you been fined, and why have you not paid your fines." I answered, "I was fined because Christian meetings take place in our house. I haven't paid because I didn't feel that I was guilty. "But you know that no religious gatherings should be held in your house. And above all it is not permitted to have children present. Why have you disobeyed the commandment of the state?" "I think that I have had the right to invite whomever I want to have in my house. I don't bother myself about other people who they invite to their houses, whether they are drinkers or not, therefore, I am of the opinion that nobody needs to be bothered about who comes to my house. And besides that we don't do anything bad!"

Upon hearing this the women judge was very excited, "So you're not doing anything bad, uh? You are destroying the children, and then you say we aren't doing anything wrong!" Now, my husband could not remain still any longer and he said, "Most respected judge Mrs. Kathaewa, you say that we are destroying the children. I ask you and the other two offi-

181

cials who have punished my wife with fines; have you ever thought of my own children while I was in prison?" Then they all remained quiet. "Please tell me if you have thought of them at least once! Of many times I will not even ask!" Once again they said nothing. "Now please tell us!" "No!" said one of the officials very shortly. My husband answered, "But my Brethren and Sisters in the faith have kept my family alive while I was in prison. Otherwise, when I got out of prison I could have looked for all of them underground. So who is destroying the children, you or we!? Who have you punished or fined for having put me into prison, me or my children? Have you ever even reflected on this? You say, we are doing everything for the children because they are the future of our country. But you don't even really think once of the children!"

This was too much for the woman judge, and she said, "Aah, you don't know anything except how to praise your Brethren!" "Naturally", said my husband. "Should we praise you since you have not looked on our children even once.?" "Yes." she said, "And you also have connections with foreigners! How can you accept packages from foreign countries?" "What should we do with them then?" asked my husband. "You should send them all back again!" she said. "No that would not be right! Should my children starve to death? Since I am at home again I have written to those who were thinking of my wife in my absence and thanked them heartily and shared with them that I am now able once more to support my own family." "But this means that you are making the Soviet Union appear bad in the eyes of foreigners, as though we didn't have enough to take care of our people ourselves? And how come you have not paid the fine money? Doesn't it say in your Bibles that you should be submissive to your rulers?" — "Are we not then submissive? We have paid our taxes and such like. But how come you never give us any receipt for the fines that have been paid? You don't pay anything without getting a receipt! Even in the post office one gets a receipt when they deliver a package. But for these fines there is no receipt!" "Isn't there?" asked the woman judge. "No, that's right, there is no receipt for such things." Then the judge looked at the other officials and said, "You mean you don't give any receipts for those who pay fines?" "No," answered they. "And why not?" "Because they already know for what they have paid!" "Normally, however, you must always give a receipt!" "Why, why should they deserve a receipt?" answered two of them. Thereupon, my husband spoke up again, "Do you ever pay anything without getting a receipt? You also know for what you are paying, and despite that you demand a receipt."

This is the way the conversation went for a while and then we finally had to leave the room. After a time we were called in again. The conclusion was: "Your fine must be paid in ten days, or else ... ?" When we were going out one of the officials said to us, "Now let your Brethren help you!" We drove home but to this day we have never paid those fines. At home we discussed what they could do to us. We began to wonder whether they could take away our sewing machine? our chest of drawers? our things purchased with gifts from abroad? or our cassette reorder? But after the ten days waiting, nobody came. A month later my husband met one of the officials in the neighboring village and this man said to him, "Mr. Hamm, I have the papers with me. I can come to you any day." With that he pointed to his briefcase and indicated that the order to pay the fines would be good for a year. But it never was presented to us. This also we attributed to God's gracious help. He never abandoned us in the hard time.

Chapter 16

An Accident

On a rainy day in July, 1969, we could not go to work in the collective farms, and my husband was at home. I, myself, was on leave because of the imminent birth of our 10th child. On this day we wanted to go into the market and buy apples. We traveled with our motorcycle. On a sharp curve on which a high hedge obscured our vision, we suddenly came up against a small truck traveling in our lane, and we crashed together. With this crash I was hurled against a pile of concrete and cement blocks. When I came to consciousness again, my husband and the driver of the truck picked me up, but I could not stand on my own feet. Fortunately, a car stopped and the driver took me to the hospital. Also my husband traveled with me.

The one physician was away on vacation and the other was making house calls. So there were only a couple nurses there who gave me an injection against the pain, and then left me lying in the corridor. Since the one physician didn't return, they finally got around to x-raying my foot and laid me on a bed. My husband traveled home meanwhile, to take care of the children.

After a short time a nurse came back and said, "The x-ray didn't turn out so you have to come and have it made again." I was now having terrible pains and I said, "I cannot go!" "I will lead you," said the nurse, "for we cannot carry you; it would be too heavy for us." As I stood up everything became black before my eyes and I had to sit down again. The long way on crutches going down the six steps and then across the court yard and across two irrigation canals was a torment for me. The nurse helped me as well as she could, but I had terrible pains and I was dizzy, and I trembled in my whole body. Finally we came to the other building. Once again I had to climb up 6 steps. The return was just as terrible a matter. Finally I lay back in my bed and felt as if I had been torn on a wheel.

After a while the nurse came again and said, "You have to be x-rayed again, because it does not show the broken ankle very well on this picture." The x-ray nurse was drunk and had taken the picture incorrectly. For that I must endure these torments once again? I said, "No! That's impossible! I am not going to do it again. Only if my husband comes and helps me." She notified my husband and he came. We had to take the x-ray pictures for the third time.

What I suffered there in pains I will never forget for my whole life. The rest of that day I had to keep on lying still without a single doctor looking at me. And of course, for this the other sick persons became unpleasant. My husband stood outside the window for he could not come into the sick room. The other patients called to my husband, "You must take your wife out of here and take her to a bone specialist. Her foot must be straightened somehow. She cannot lie here groaning the whole night long. And we can't bear it to hear her or even look at her!"

Thereupon my husband hurried to the nurse and asked her where I should be brought. But the nurse declined saying, "I cannot allow that, otherwise they will remove me from my job. What should I live from then! No, I cannot allow that!" "But it can't continue on like this! I cannot allow it that anyone treats my wife in this way!" said my husband. "Well then, go yourself to the doctor who is on vacation. He hasn't really gone away anywhere. Up there in the house by the court yard is his house. Perhaps he can do something." My husband ran there. But the doctor would not undertake anything and also would not allow my husband to take me elsewhere. Then my husband became impatient and said, "Now I am going to take her from here by force and drive to Frunza. The kinds of things you are doing here are not permitted!" After that he came to me and spoke through the window. Have patience, I am going now to the crossroad to fetch a taxi to take you to Frunza. (Our motorcycle could of course not be used because of the accident).

After some time, the Doctor stirred himself and came after all and gave me an injection. He began pulling on my foot in order to reset it. And with that it cracked! Then he went away again. After this I had to vomit heftily. Finally my husband came back. He had neither car nor taxi, nor even a motorcycle, although he had gone up and down on many streets, and looked in vain.

In the next days my foot was finally put into plaster and after a week I came home again. I had to remain in bed since I could not walk because of the pain. Shortly after that, I went to the women's clinic and was there delivered of our youngest child-a boy. What I suffered in these days for pains is impossible to describe in words. In the woman's clinic, my foot was also x-rayed and the doctor said to me, "But the bone is completely splintered. It is no wonder that you had such frightful pains!"

For eight long months I had to go on crutches. We had visited many other doctors and all tried to somehow help this foot to improve. We even went 800 kilometers away to Duschanbe in Turkestan. Our congregation helped us so that we could buy the airplane ticket.

Often I had to think on the words, "Lord, if you were not my consolation where could I have gone in my misery. (Psalm 119:92). Many of our friends and Brethren and Sisters visited me in my time of sickness and consoled me with the Word of God. They faithfully prayed for me and I have only God to thank that I can walk once more.

On the 29th of April, 1978, we had another accident in which I broke a bone in the other foot. Here in the Federal Republic of Germany, I was, however, well cared for by the doctors. As to pains, I did not have to suffer even once, a tenth of what I suffered in the USSR.

Chapter 17

Abram: You Can't Limp on Both Legs

When I was released from the concentration camp in November, 1968, I hoped that our congregation would be spared somewhat from this point on. But this was not to be so. Over and over it came to new court hearings, and money fines were assessed. Seeking always stricter regulations, the government teachers had to visit our congregation to control and investigate and report. The surrounding congregations of Pokrowka, Jurjewka and Kant had been spared arrests, even though they held meetings and persuaded youth groups, but we in Iwanowka were not left in peace. We had often asked ourselves why that should be so. According to our own opinion we were not worse, and also not better than the other congregations. But since 1975, the picture changed. In these other congregations Brethren and Sisters were also arrested; and in Iwanowka, on the contrary, no others were taken until 1985.

After my return from the concentration camp I was chosen once again as a helper of the leading Brethren by the congregation. During my time in the camp, Walter Willms had been installed as leader; so now there were two of us as helpers. Edward Bormann had led the youth work and now was involved in it once again. As soon as I had come back home again, I was summoned before School Committee, which was composed of teachers and some parents. I thought that it was a matter of my children and their scholastic accomplishments. But this was not the reason. I was sharply attacked and asked why my children had not joined the Communist Pioneers group. I replied, "According to the law this is a voluntary matter!" Then the teacher answered, "Of course it is a voluntary matter; but we of the school all desire to see that our scholars belong to the government youth movement!" Then the following proposal was made, "We will give Abram Hamm two weeks of time to think it over. If he has not changed his mind then, he shall be sent into exile!" Others proposed to give me two months of time to think it over. Then I was asked for my opinion. I replied, "As a believing father, I cannot enroll my children in a godless organization which even according to the law is required to work against the believers. So long as my eyes are open and my tongue moves I will always say, "No! I can do nothing else!"

Then once again like hail, statements rained down upon me. "You've already been arrested once and put into the concentration camp. But that apparently has not yet cured you! In fact, you have not improved at all. It seems like you don't want to learn!"

The chairman of this committee was Brother D. R. from the registered church! I could tell by looking at him that he did not feel good about presiding over this kind of affair, in which he was required to condemn a Brother. But when anyone allows his church to be registered then he is putting himself in the situation where it is possible to work against other believers.

Now it had to be voted on what was going to happen to me. This had not yet been decided, whether I should get two weeks or two months of time to think it over. The chairman asked, "Who is in favor of this that Abram Hamm should be exiled if he does not change? Raise your hand!" I thought, What will the unhappy Brother do now who is put on the spot by this question? Will he lift his hand against his Brother and condemn him? I did not look at the other members of the committee, only at the chairman. Slowly he raised his hand, scratched himself on the cheek and then proceeded to count the other lifted hands.

Then one of the committee members made an interruption, and said, "We cannot vote! Because it has not yet been decided whether he has one or two months of time to think it over!" Now the argument began again. Some were for two months, but the others said, "Two weeks are long enough! We are being plagued the whole year long with him taking this position. It is just not necessary. Let's put an end to it!" But they could not come to a united decision. After a long discussion the chairman said, "Have we now all finished speaking about the things against Hamm?" Somebody answered, "Yes!" Then I asked, "May I go now?" He said, "Yes!" Immediately I stood up and went out cheerfully. After that nothing happened to me until my arrest in October of 1970.

Chapter 18

House Search, Arrest, And Trial

After the action of the school committee, our congregation grew ever larger. Several more people were converted and baptized. We experienced days rich in blessing. Certainly there were also many difficulties and struggles. And those will always be found in our life of faith. The accuser of the Brethren is always at work and never lets the believers at peace. He would like to extinguish faith in Jesus Christ, and for that purpose he has willing instruments. But his goal will not be successful; for Jesus is, and always will be, the victor.

In July of 1970, my wife traveled with some of our children to visit our relatives in Orenburg. During the time that she was away, I devoted myself to making many repairs inside and outside of our house. In two rooms I varnished the floor. The varnish, however, was not really good and dried very slowly; so that by the time of my birthday on the fifth of August, I still could not step on these floors.

Right after I had eaten my breakfast that day in the kitchen, an official car drove by and two men and three women got out. They came in and showed me an order to search my house. My children knew what they had to do. Immediately they hid some writings and ran to the house of the elder of our congregation. Underway they met his children and learned that a search was also underway at their house. As we learned later on; this same morning in at least seven different houses at one time, government searches were being made.

During this house search I was not allowed to leave the kitchen. One of the officials sat beside me and the others rummaged through everything and threw things on the floor. In the two rooms with the still wet varnish they could of course not enter. So they took the window out from outside, shoved boards over the floor and succeeded in this way to enter the rooms in order to search the closets.

Finally they took spades and dug up the garden in different places. I didn't know what they were looking for. Certainly I did not have any weapons or munitions, nor any gold and silver treasures. Now it became apparent that what they were actually looking for, was spiritual literature. Almost everything that I had of that, plus, the copy machine that I had been using, with which I copied Bible verses, they took with them. The most hurtful thing was that they took my Russian and German Bibles and confiscated them. Upon my repeated pleas, I did later get my German Bible back.

One of the officials photographed me in the room and then outside, from all sides, and then in concluding even took a photo of me beside the auto. I invited him to send me a copy of the picture, which he promised, but never fulfilled.

At the homes of the seven other members of the congregation, a host of things were confiscated, especially at Jacob Mekelberger's house. His wife Toni and Maria Rempel had secretly prepared a concordance to be printed. The leading Brethren of our church knew nothing of this; only that in the congregation somewhere a secret book-bindery was in operation.

Since Maria Rempel and Edward Bormann had been shepherding the growing youth, both of them were arrested; Maria Rempel at the end of August and Edward Bormann at the beginning of September. And at the end of September our leading Brother, Isaac Dück was also arrested and taken into custody. In spite of it all, the work of the congregation, including children's and youth work, continued on. In October we even celebrated a baptismal service.

Initially I still hoped that I would not be arrested. But when I was summoned to a hearing at the beginning of October, I thought, Now they have come to my turn! At the trial I was ordered to speak out against Maria Rempel, Isaac Dück, and Edward Bormann. I answered, "I will not let myself be made into a Judas." Then the investigative judge was angry and screamed at me, "Don't you know that you are just making it worse for yourself?" I replied, "Yes, I know that. But despite that, I will still not let myself be made into a Judas! Lock me up in jail rather."

By the next hearing I was not called anymore, but as one of those who is accused. I had to sign a certificate that I would not leave the community until after the court trial.

On the twentieth of October, 1970, Walter Willms and I were ordained as elders by Jacob Günter. On the same day I received a summons from the investigative judge; a summons to come on the 21st of October to Tokmok. I traveled there but the investigative judge was not present, so then I traveled back home again. In the evening about six o'clock, the militia police appeared and demanded that I present myself, be ready with warm clothing, and bring along something to eat. They said no word about arrest so that the children would not weep and cry, but I knew what was happening. My wife called all the children together. Some of them had been playing outside and brought neighboring children along with them inside, and I said, "Children, we want to pray." They were startled, but said nothing. Then I knelt down with them and prayed in the Russian language. I prayed for my wife and my children, for our congregation and also for my persecutors. With that the militia police drew softly back into the kitchen, but let the door open and listened without speaking. Then I took leave of my family. Our youngest, Peter, only a year and two months old, sat on the arm of my wife and waved good-bye to me in a friendly manner. He could not expect that he would not see me again until three years later.

In the militia auto I was taken to Tokmak and put in investigative imprisonment. Some days later I was taken to the main prison in Frunza, the capital of Kirgisia. This happened a few times back and forth. As we were suddenly taken from Frunza to the court appearance in Tokmak, I met the Brethren Dück and Bormann again in the train. We would have been glad to stay together, but in Tokmak we were put into separate cells. After that I prayed, "Lord, if you want you can bring it about that I will be put together with Brother Dück and Brother Bormann." After about ten minutes an overseer came into our cell and said, "Who would like to leave here and go into another cell? There are too many in this one." I didn't blink an eyelash, but immediately volunteered. I thought, I'm going to lose nothing by volunteering like this and I might gain, being put together with the Brethren. The overseer went along the long hallway, then he opened the cell and stuck me in it. Nine other men were already in it, and—a miracle! Brother Dück and Brother Bormann were with them! Great joy filled me. I thanked my Lord, that he had so wonderfully cared for his own, that even in this hell of a communist prison in concentration camp, we were not alone. Actually, the legal restrictions did not even allow it for prisoners accused of the same crime to be put into the same cell before the court trial. But here the Lord had so overruled.

The other prisoners were curious to know on what grounds we three had been locked up. We testified to them that we were here because of our faith in the living Jesus, who loves us, and had given his life for us, so that with it we would be free of all guilt and have an eternal hope. It was because of this assurance that we were in prison. We sang and prayed together and quoted Bible verses from memory. With that, we had to lament how few actually we had in our memories. This also had occurred to me during my first imprisonment.

During the hearing, the investigative judge said to me, "You really are stupid! Just think of your wife and your children. Do you want to leave them to misery because they no longer have support? Your wife can no longer work because of the many children, and she receives very little money. From that they cannot live! You don't need to really promise that you will renounce your faith; just promise that you will obey the laws of the state which specify that teaching children and young people, so as to influence them religiously, is a forbidden activity! And why don't you want your congregation to become registered? You know Romans the 13th chapter where it is written "Obey them that have the rule over you!" This was not an easy matter to answer; but the more I thought over it, the more I came to the conviction that I could not come to such a compromise with the state, and that I would not sign any such articles that were clearly against God's expressed will. He has commanded us to preach the Gospel to all men, also to children and youths.

As the trial date neared, I asked my Brethren in the faith with what kind of punishment they thought we would be sentenced. Brother Dück thought, "They will probably give me two years." And Brother Bormann said, "I also calculate that I will get up to two years." "And what do you think?" they asked me. "I'll probably get three years," answered I. All three of us had guessed well. It came out exactly that way.

Chapter 19

Court Procedure in Pokrowka

The court case took place from the 23rd to the 25th of November, 1970, in Pokrowka. Many spectators sat in the courtroom; most of them were believers. We three Brethren sat together with Maria Rempel up front on the bench for the accused. This time too, the presiding judge was Mrs. Kathaewa. A Kirgisian attorney was present even though I had renounced the privilege of having him defend me, and had instead chosen to defend myself. How could he indeed have thought to defend a Christian; really defend him and thereby put his own career in danger! The State's Prosecuting Attorney, the Defense Attorney, and the Judge were actually all of the same convictions. Even before the process, they had most probably spoken among one another as to how the course of the case would be run, and what kind of punishment would be hung on us. They accused us of religiously influencing children and youth and of having founded a Sunday School for children.

During one pause in the case, we four accused had to leave the courtroom and were led into another room under guard. There we knelt down and thanked the Lord that we were able to bear witness for him during this case. The guards granted us this permission.

The witnesses in the case who were to be heard after the recess, presented lying testimony. They knew anyway that they would not be made liable for perjury. To the contrary they hoped that they would be awarded for it by the KGB officials.

One witness by the name of Saschien, spoke up to say that I had kidnapped a young man and forced him to attend the worship service. Supposedly he was named Waldemar Bormann. This young man was present in the courtroom and cried loudly, "That is not true. Nobody forced me to go to the worship service! I went completely of my own will!" He was not a believer, but these flagrant lies had so irritated him that he could not remain silent. He was driven out of the court room.

My wife told me later what had happened during the recess when we were absent. After the State Prosecuting Attorney had shared with the spectators what kind of punishment would be directed against us, the spectators had shouted, "That's much too little! Why are you trifling any longer with these people? Away with them! Not only for three years, but for ten or twenty years; lock them up! You should put an end to them so that we would not have to listen to their pious chatter anymore!" The Prosecuting Attorney tried to quiet them with the remark, "We live, however, in a humane land; and for this reason we want to proceed mildly with them. Perhaps they may come to their senses yet and improve."

It was cast up to me especially what I had said during an earlier hearing. At that time I had explained, "You probably could lock us up, or even kill us, but you are fighting against the living God and his congregation; and you are fighting in vain. If you lock one of us up, two others will rise in his place. And if you lock these two up, then there will be four new ones coming to take their place, and when you lock up these four, eight more will appear. For the things that we are doing are not the things of men, but of God."

On the third day, before the Judge returned to give the sentence, we that were accused were permitted a final word. I explained, "We must all come before the eternal and just God as our judge on the last day. Then each one will be judged, just as he has deserved. No innocent person will be condemned. But neither will the guilty be freed. Many who are mocking today will experience the truth of the Word of God in that day. It says, "It is a fearful thing to fall into the hands of the living God!" (Heb 10:31) Then I was interrupted with the cry, "Don't preach to us! Come to the point!"

With certainty the case neared its end. After the sentence was spoken nobody was permitted to speak even a word with me, but my wife and children did it anyhow. My daughter, Maria, even stuck some chocolates into my pocket. I would rather not have taken the chocolates with me because our children hardly ever received anything like that; but Maria did so much want to do something for me, and for this reason I accepted it. Next we were driven very quickly into the police van at the entrance to the building, and no one could take leave of us or say "Good-bye." A few people threw chocolates into our van, including even Waldemar Bormann. When the police noticed this they grabbed him and shoved him into the van, too. Only at the police station and jail was he released again. But later, because of this gift of chocolates, he was sentenced to a year in prison in the strictest custody. The reason for this is, in the Soviet Union it is not permitted to be humane to prisoners.

In the van as the chocolates fell into my lap I thought, If they ever find these they will confiscate them at once. But since it was dark in the van, nobody could see that I stuck two packets of chocolates into my socks. The other two I left in my pocket. Before we came into the prison cells, we were searched thoroughly; and they took everything away from us. Only the chocolates in our socks were not found, so I could keep them. In the cell Brother Dück and Brother Bormann said, "They have taken away the chocolate from us!" Then I jokingly asked them, "You mean you like to eat chocolate?" "But of course! and I wonder where they take those?" "Just a minute," said I, "I'll give you each a piece." And I reached down into my sock and got the chocolate for them. Brother Dück said smilingly, "You sly one, you are more clever than we!" I answered, "When you have been arrested for the second time, then you become more clever!" So we ate these chocolates with much consolation and even gave some to other prisoners.

Then the next day we complained to the police chief that chocolates had been stolen from us. We said, "If we ourselves are not permitted to have them, then we would have wanted to give them to the children at least. Naturally, we accomplished nothing with them. That kind of rights were not expected for prisoners.

Chapter 20

In The Punishment Camp At Nowopokrowka

After a two week stay in the jail in Frunza, I came into the concentration camp of Nowopokrowka, a place of very strict guard, between Frunza and Kant. It was especially for backsliding prisoners, those who had not improved. Only twice a month were we permitted to write a letter. And only twice a year could we have visitors. In the camps under the ordinary guard, to which Brother D×uck and Brother Bormann were sent, one could write letters as often as one wanted, and visitors were allowed four times a year.

In our first visit we were allowed one or two days with our relatives. But the second time it was terrible. Then we were led into a large room inside of which was a smaller room (so called the aquarium) with high wooden walls and thick transparent glass standing between the prisoner and his family. On the walls of this room, inside and out, there were many telephone booths built. The prisoners were first led into the aquarium and the door closed and locked behind them. Thereupon, the relatives were permitted to go into the outer room. They went around the aquarium until they found the place where their own relative was seated opposite them. Then with the help of the telephone they could speak with one another for two hours. It was impossible to hear a single sound without the telephone. The mother lifted her children up so that the father could see their faces at least. The conversation was always monitored by the guards, especially that of prisoners whose name was on the black list. And it was also required that all conversations be conducted in Russian.

After two hours the telephones were cut off, one could only make gestures to the loved one. And then they had to leave and later also the prisoners. I only experienced this type of meeting once, and then no more;

since in the middle of my sentence I was taken away for five months and ten days to work outside on construction work at a distance from the camp.

A believing Brother by the name of Erwin Dreger, who often came into the camp as a free man in order to work there, had given me a small Russian New Testament and I guarded it as if it were a precious gem. Also I often felt pressed in the spirit to read from it to other prisoners. In the camp we had iron beds which were placed on top of one another in order to accommodate more prisoners. I slept in the topmost bed. In the lower bunks lay Wasja, who had lost a leg during the war. His assigned task was to keep the concentration camp school clean. This school was used for those prisoners who had little or no education. One day Wasja asked me, "Abram, do you have anything to read in Russian?" He knew that I was a German and a Christian. I showed him my New Testament and said, "This you can read. Whatever you don't understand just ask me. I will explain it to you. But take good care of it so that no guard sees it. Otherwise it will be gone forever. It is very, very valuable to me!" He promised, "Yes, yes! Good, I will take good care of it!" Then he hurried to the concentration Camp School to have a place where he could read. The next morning we had to line up as usual and were counted. Since one was missing we were counted again, and then for a third time. Actually, someone was missing. So a search was undertaken. Finally they found Wasja. He had fallen asleep and for this reason was put into solitary confinement. I was shocked and thought, My New Testament! Now its gone! At first I wanted to console myself with the thought that perhaps Wasja did not have it with him. But a few hours later I was called in by the secret police. Then I knew what was wrong. They had found the New Testament and now it was lost to me. Even worse was the thought, they will ask me where I got it! What shall I say? I dare not betray the Brother who had brought it into the camp, otherwise he would lose his work! But neither could I lie! On the way to the hearing I prayed, "Lord Jesus, I cannot betray the Brother, and to lie is something that I cannot do either. So please direct the hearing that I do not need to say the whole truth, but also that I do not need to lie." With that confidence that the Lord alone can give to human hearts, and that he can overrule and turn them like a water brook I stepped into the office.

The officer greeted me politely and bade me take a seat. Then my unrest disappeared somewhat. The first question was: "Is this your New Testament?" I affirmed that it was. "Now then, how did this come into the concentration camp." God gave it to me at that point to speak up cheerfully and say, "Ach, my dear Commissar, what all does not come into these camps! Here a person could even bring a cannon in, how much more easily a little book?" Then he laughed out loud and said, "Do you think so?" "But of course! Here one really should not have any money with him, but many do have it non-the-less. Nobody should have drugs or opium, but many have them anyhow. And so it goes with many other things, too." He agreed with this and said, "You are right!"

Then I began to speak of the New Testament in order to divert him from the question he had put to me. I said, "The New Testament is such a good book, it doesn't teach anything bad. I would like to have it back again. It is not really any kind of a crime to own one. Because here in the Soviet Union we have religious freedom." He listened to all of this and did not ask any more questions about how it had come into the camp. The New Testament, however, I never did get back which is what I expected.

During the first four months in the concentration camp I still had no Bible. So I helped myself with Christian devotional books which my wife had received from Germany and secretly sent to me in the form of calendar pages. Among the two thousand prisoners there were about twenty who, like myself, were of German descent. But most of them could not even read German. To some I gave these calendar pages to read. Among them, Walter Vetter received a page with a short devotion that contained a verse from Revelation 3:20 which said, "Behold, I stand at the door and knock." Then the reader was asked what his condition was spiritually, and whether he had the forgiveness of sins or not, and if not, whether he would accept Christ. Through this Walter Vetter learned that Jesus was the only salvation. Hearing this he came under conviction and fell crying to his pillow asking God for forgiveness. After he had become a Christian, I gave him not only the pages of the scripture diary book, but also read with him my German Bible. This particular German Bible had an interesting story behind it. In the summer of 1970, shortly before my arrest, my family had received a little package from West Germany with a pair of little children's shoes. The shoes were filled with paper that had been balled up (rolled up). We noticed at once that these papers seemed to be pages from a Bible the size of about 14 centimeters by 10 centimeters. After we had painstakingly sorted out the pages and then ironed out the rolled up paper, which took us several hours, we found to our astonishment that we now had every page of the Bible, from the first page of Genesis to the last page of Revelation. One brother volunteered to bind together these pages, and cover them with an appropriate binding.

I was thankful for this little Bible which I could very easily carry in my pocket. If our services were interrupted by the KGB, this Bible could easily be hidden from them. In the concentration camp I had it with me for almost three years. During this time it became ever more dear to me. At the time of our emigration from Russia in 1974, to West Germany, I wanted to take it along with me. But it did not seem right that I should take it back to where it had come from. So I presented it to Brother B. Giesbrecht from our congregation in Iwanowka. Seven years later, however, I received it into my hands once again. I sent the Brother two other Bibles in exchange for it. I am very glad now to have this little Bible here in the West to give as evidence of what we went through back there. Maybe I will meet the person someday who sent us not only shoes, but also bread from heaven, and concealed the Bible in that cunning way as packing.

Walter Vetter worked in the camp tailor shop and sewed for me a little pocket with snaps where I could hide this Bible, and put it into my pillow. From outside one could see nothing in the pillow. Only if one handled it or poked it could one notice that there was a firmer substance somewhere inside. For about six months I was able to hide my Bible. Every day after work the first thing I looked for was to see if my Bible was still there.

One evening in the autumn of 1972, as we came back from work, we heard that there had been a great search throughout the camp. That came about from time to time, and seemed that hardly a nail could be concealed. At once I was afraid as I thought about my Bible. But full of wondering joy, I saw that the Bible was sticking half out of the open pillow! I was astonished that it had not been confiscated! It was a usual thing for one of the forty prisoners in the sleeping room to remain behind and watch over that room as he put it in order while the others went to work. I asked the one who had been responsible for cleaning the room that day, "Tell me actually what happened." Then he told the following, "Three soldiers of the guard came in here, three Russians and a Kirgisan. They soon noticed that something was hidden in your pillow. They cut it open and found the Bible. They could not recognize it as a Bible because it was printed in German. Then said the Kirgisan, 'With us Moslems it is also true that whenever we have anything that is very dear to us or of great value we lay it under our pillow, or stick it inside. We'll just leave this thing here.' And the two Russians were in agreement with that." So the Bible remained in my possession. The joy that I had from it cannot be described!

I would like to tell one more experience that I had with my Bible. Walter Vetter and I looked for a place where we could read the Bible undisturbed. For this reason we once climbed on top of the roof of a half finished barrack building. Walter read and I explained the text. We had made the agreement that whoever was listening had to keep his eyes open to see if any guard was coming so that we could hide the Bible. However, if a guard would surprise us and discover the Bible, we would not undertake anything, but just wait and see what would happen. We were so deeply involved in our reading that we never noticed when a lieutenant of the guards suddenly approached us. Only when he stood directly before us that I said to Walter, "There is somebody; it is too late to hide the Bible!" The Lieutenant screamed, "What are you doing here? Ha! You are reading the Bible! Does it belong to you Hamm?" "Yes," said I, "That is my Bible!" "Give it to me!" It was very hard for me to give it up. But what else could I do? I was powerless! I begged him, "Walera, give me my Bible back!" "No, come along with me now to the hearing. If you get it back there, well and good!" That I would never be able to get it back again, was now clear to me. For this reason I still begged a couple of times for my Bible. But he said, "Nothing doing! Follow me!"

Sadly I followed the guard. In my heart I was praying, "Lord Jesus, please let me have this Bible. You have protected it so wonderfully up to now. Please, keep on doing it." Meanwhile we came to the steps. When we were halfway down the steps, I saw one of the Superior Officers. He immediately saw what was up. He saw the Bible in the hand of the Lieutenant and me sadly coming behind him. I knew this Superior Officer because outside of my work time I had often done favors for him. For example, I had to be responsible to give out the tools in the morning and then in the evening collect them and put them in order again; and the Superior Officer who was building his own house outside the camp, brought me after work a few shovels, spades and axes which had broken handles so that I could repair them. Although I was not actually responsible for his tools I did this as a favor for him.

As I saw the Superior Officer standing there I thought, Here is somebody who can help me. I pointed to him with both hands, and then to the Lieutenant, and then last to myself. That should signify, "Please tell the Lieutenant that he should give my Bible back again." He understood my signal immediately, for as we approached him he said to the Lieutenant, "Give him the book!" "How so?" replied he. "We are just now going to the office for a hearing. If he can keep the book after that hearing then that will be OK." He had hardly said this though, when the Superior Officer replied shortly, "Give him the book!" The Lieutenant had to obey because a higher officer had commanded him. Now it was happening to him like it happened to me on the roof before. But only very slowly did he give me my Bible back and said, "If I find you with it once more, your Bible will be disposed of forever." I thought, Only if God permits you!

In the year 1970, the new amnesty was pronounced in celebration of the fiftieth anniversary of the entry of the Kirgisian Republic into the Soviet Republic. One of the clauses stated: "Whoever has been condemned for the second time and only for three years or less does not need to remain in the concentration camp but only in exile, and that not in Siberia or the icy regions of the north, but in the city of Tokmok!" Since that was only three kilometers away from my village of Iwanowka, I was very happy. Those in exile had the permission to visit their families and to receive visitors. In the place of their exile they could go about freely and visit some of the stores. Also they did not need to appear regularly to be counted. Thus it was naturally much better than being in a concentration camp where one was hemmed in by barbed wire walls and guard posts with guns and surrounded by fierce dogs; where one was always watched and counted three times a day. In exile, conditions were much better. The prisoner had to earn for himself his clothing and his food. And half of his wages were taken by the state. The prisoner was limited to only five rubles a month, and could be spent for such things as pen, paper and stamps; if he had extra money he could buy a little margarine or some cheap candy, and if the money would reach that far a can of fish or additional bread.

I thought, I hope that I will now be included in this amnesty. I owned a motorcycle at home and wanted to fetch it so that I could travel home oftener to visit. But this time I was bitterly disappointed. I had to hear once more, "You have not improved yourself." Now it was forbidden to me to pray, to read the Bible, and especially to mention Jesus Christ and his Gospel to any of the other prisoners. But those were all commandments to which I could not submit myself. Had not my Lord commanded that we should preach the Gospel to every creature? So there we stood; I had not improved myself, and the amnesty would not be for me. It was good for robbers, thieves, and murderers, but not for Christians!

Chapter 21

Work and Visits Outside The Camp

As the first year of my three year's punishment came to an end, the commissar of our brigade made the following known:— whoever has served a third of his sentence has the option of working in Beskonwojka. That meant that during the day one could work outside of the camp without armed guards. Also it meant that friends and relatives could be seen oftener and also more nourishing food could be received from home. Since I now had a third of my sentence behind me this filled me with great hope. But at the same time this thought presented itself: "How can this apply to me? Just think how it was with the amnesty of 1967 and that of 1970. Then I was told, "You, as a believer, do not come under the amnesty. You have not improved yourself or reformed. You are worse than a bandit! You are not included in this!"

In spite of that I decided to try and see if I could receive this option. The list of those who were signing up for this option went through the whole camp. I decided to sign up. If I were denied then at least I had done what I could. I wrote nothing about this to my wife because I did not want to awaken any hope in her which would later be disappointed. During this time I was working as a "Banschik." That means I had to get bath things for the prisoners ready and keep them clean and in good order; which included the bath room and the bath house to be kept in clean condition. About four hours a day I had to do this work. And it was not hard. I also had to be present on Saturdays and Sundays, and keep my eye on the pipes and plumbing and make sure that hot water was at hand; because Saturdays after work, and Sundays were wash days for all the prisoners. On the other days of the week only people with special permits could use the bathing rooms.

These eight months working as a "Banschik" were the most agreeable time of my camp experience. From Monday to Friday I could be alone in the rooms and shut the door behind me. In one of these days each week a loud voice from outside would shout: "Believer, Believer! The officer of the secret service wants to bathe. Open up!" Actually, officially he was not permitted to bathe here, but he did it anyway because he did not have to pay here. One had to pay in the city. (In the USSR in those times very few people had any bathing facilities in their own homes).

While the officer washed himself I sat in the dressing room at a little table, sang my songs and accompanied myself with the guitar which I had borrowed from another prisoner. "What kind of beautiful songs those are! Are those Christian songs?" "Yes." Then he confessed, "You know my parents were also believers." We often discussed questions of faith, and I soon noticed that it was having an effect. One day he asked me, "Haven't you signed a petition for that option of working outside the camp in Beskonwojnik?" I said, "Yes," but added, "however it will all be in vain." "Now," he said, "We'll see about that. I'll do what I can to get it accepted for you."

It was just in those days that the prisoner Walter Vetter had come to belief in Jesus Christ. Through some other prisoners who had close contacts with the leadership of the camp, I learned shortly afterwards that they had said, "We're going to have to do something about this Hamm." Then my hope disappeared of ever getting out of the camp. Yet I prayed, "Lord, if you will, I can get out of here and then it will happen, even though it looks like it's impossible."

Something else happened about this same time. Prisoners from the camp punishment cells were being led in to be washed. They were like starved wolves and begged me, "Please give us something to eat." Or, "Get a message to my friends to bring me something." The latter thing I could not do; but I did give them something to eat because it was pitiful to see how starved they were. Some of them were drug-addicted and their friends tried everything to get drugs to them.

On the next day I was summoned to the camp office. The Chief screamed at me, "What have you done?" I answered, "Nothing." "Yes, you have been giving opium and morphine to those prisoners. When they were brought back to their cells we searched through their things and found it. But no one had any access to them except you." I answered, "Out of pity I have given them some of our own food. But I have never had anything to do with drugs." "How then could they have come back from

the bath house with something like that? That must have been something
that you did." I maintained my innocence but nobody believed me. Then
the officials set up a placard stating that I was fired as bath master and
would be punished.

After that I hurried back to the washroom and searched everything
closely. Soon I discovered that in the wall beside where the pipes came in
there was a hole big enough so that someone could stick something
through it. It led through the wall to the room where the hot water heaters
stood. So someone from this room must have been able to put the drugs
through the hole in the wall into the bathing room.

At this moment the secret service officer went by who had often used
the bathing facilities. I begged him to look at this thing. He examined it
and said, "Now this is completely clear. I will see to it that this threat of
punishment against you will be canceled." Then I was glad of this because I myself had already experienced the punishment cells.

Finally the day came in which of the two thousand prisoners, twelve
would be chosen to work outside the camp. In my heart there still
gleamed a little spark of hope. I prayed again, "You can make all things
possible. But I don't know whether it is good for me, and I want to do
what you want me to do. I will accept whatever comes."

Then I heard over the loud speaker that twelve names were being read
out. I could hardly make myself understand. But my own name was
among them! The announcement was repeated! It was a fact! I had not
misunderstood! We were all ordered to come to the camp office and to
bring our passes. It seemed to me as though my heart wanted to spring out
of my breast, and I prayed, "Oh Lord, how I thank you for this goodness!" At the same time I was plagued with this thought, Maybe I won't
be at this kind of work for very long. But in any case I determined that the
time the Lord will permit me to be outside I would use for him.

It was the 10th of February, 1972, when the twelve of us were led out of
the camp in order to strengthen the work brigades that worked outside.
On the afternoon of this day I was supposed to have received a visit from
my friends. My joy about this whole thing was very great. The hours proceeded much too slowly until this great event could take place. Again and
again I looked at the building where my wife should arrive. How her eyes
would get big when she saw me waiting outside because she knew nothing
of it. About 4:00 o'clock Samuel Rose drove up on his motorcycle with a
side car and stopped. My wife and our three smallest children climbed
out. My heart beat for joy. I went up to them and they were astonished!

"Indeed can that be Papa? It has to be! And look, he is even outside of the camp. How did this ever happen?" "This is something that our God has done!"

In the building in which the prisoners were allowed to meet with their relatives, there was a room set aside for us. Many times it happened that it would also be free the next day and those in charge, if they were in a good mood, would then allow one to be together with the visitors this second day. And this is how it happened. We were happy that we could be together for two days. And the hours went by very rapidly. From then on, I could receive a visit from my wife every week, and not only from her, but also from the children!

It just seemed to me that even the very air outside the camp was much better than in the concentration camp. Every time that I had the opportunity to go outside the heavy iron gate and be among free men once more, I was filled with thanksgiving and joy.

One day the secret service officer, who had visited the bath when I was in charge there, came again to me. He asked, "Well now, how is it going?" "Wonderfully," I answered. Then he told me how it had happened when my name was being discussed on whether to include me in the outside work detail. Half of the committee was against me. But he himself had put in a good word for me. Then the Chief of the camp whose word was decisive in questionable matters had said, "We need him outside." Further, the officer said to me, "When you get visitors, come to me and report it and then every thing will go smoothly."

Here outside the camp the number of short visits was not restricted for us. but we still had to report either to our overseer, or to one of the Secret Service Officials. The prisoners with whom I worked seldom if ever received any visits, because their relatives lived much too far away or else were dead.

My fellow believers from different congregations in the community often sought me out and prayed with me. They came so often that the Brethren from my own congregation advised me, "You'll have to restrict yourself. They dare not come so often or you will be locked up again in the camp." I answered them, "I am doing nothing against it. May it last as long as it can. It could be that I won't be outside the camp for very long anyway. I am hoping for at least two months. I am regarding this as a leave that the Lord has given me."

During the first week a KGB captain from the camp, by the name of Kowalenko, came to me. He had often tried before to persuade me that

there was no God. For this purpose he brought me books in which it wa
supposedly proven that God does not exist. Among them was one i
which the space astronaut Urie Gagarin had told how that he had flow
higher and higher and had never seen any sign of God. I said to Kowa
lenko: "Gagarin flew much too low. What is the distance he traveled i
comparison with the universe! He has only hopped as high as a flea. Be
sides, it stands written in the Word of God that we cannot see God. W
live now in faith but we shall see him when we come to eternity."

Then Kowalenko began to trot forth the sins of Abraham and Lot an
Jacob and David, as though to say those were some saints indeed! I an
swered him, "But exactly those reports show me that the Bible is genuin
and true. It portrays humanity as it is and really was. It doesn't conceal o
spare us anything as your worldly historians do. They represent the lead
ers and politicians as though they were all noble and good persons with
out mistakes and weaknesses. But this is something the Bible never does
It tells the truth."

Since Kowalenko couldn't say anything more about that, he came up
with the flood, with Jonah, with the resurrection, with the walking on the
water of the sea and with other miracles, and spoke about these things tha
were hard to believe. I said to him in reply, "If we could explain all o
these things in a rational way, then they would not be miracles. I believe
what is written, for the Bible says the truth."

Then Kowalenko maintained that my reason was so darkened, and my
understanding so ignorant that he could do nothing more to help me.
From that time on he sought no more to dissuade me. When he saw me
here, standing and working outside the camp, he was greatly surprised
and exclaimed, "And how come you are here outside also? How can that
be possible?" Then I replied, "I heard that you were the leader of the
committee that made up the number of those who were to work outside."
"But no, that wasn't I. At that time I was on leave!" So wonderfully had
God led that the committee that came together at the time this was decided for me, did not include Kowalenko! Therefore, he could not have
said his "No!" and thereby deny me this privilege.

Our brigade, working outside of the camp, consisted of 22 persons.
The brigadier, who was also a prisoner and a Kirgisen, was satisfied with
me, for I understood much of construction work; whereas most of the
prisoners, even the Kirgisen himself had no experience with it. Most of
them were sheep herders and never had anything to do with house construction. In the morning I gave out the tools and in the evening collected

them again. I was also responsible for repairs and sharpening of the instruments. For this purpose I had a small room with a worktable for my use. During the remaining part of the day I helped with the construction.

The food in the camp was bad morning and evening. Only midday meal which was prepared for us and sent out of the camp was better. With it there always was borscht soup, the taste of which I liked. In the mornings we had 250 grams of bread, and midday 200 grams, and in the evening another 250 grams. These 700 grams of bread suffice as a daily ration only if it would be supplemented by meats, fats and vegetables. But there was too little meat and fat and the bread itself was badly baked and wet.

We prisoners were not allowed to speak much with the civilian population. What we would say had to be limited to only the necessary things. And what was considered to be necessary? For me it always seemed that the most necessary thing was to tell any and every person to bring his life in order with God. Without this how could the salvation of his soul be secured. For this reason I used every opportunity that presented itself to enter into conversation with people about Jesus Christ, especially if they were open to him.

While we were building the house, I came into conversation with a 60 year old German lady. She told me that six months ago she had come to belief in God, but did not own a Bible, not even a New Testament. She had begged the Brethren from a registered congregation to give her spiritual literature, but as yet she had received nothing. Since the last official printing of the Bible was in 1938, it was hard to find anymore Bibles. That was not something that seemed extraordinary. Russia does not provide Bibles for her citizens. I myself possessed a Bible, a New Testament, the book of Romans and other Bible books which we had received from Germany. Besides that I had daily devotional Bible readings from Christian calendars that had been sent to me. I had the opportunity to bring out from the prison some of this literature for the woman. How happy she was about them. You who live here in the West can never know! Here one can have enough Bibles, but actually how much of the time are people reading their Bibles? This woman had tears of joy in her eyes. She said, "Out here in freedom it is hard to get even a little bit to read. And here you are a prisoner, and bring with you something to read out of the camp!"

Sometime later Brother Reimer, from the congregation in Leninpol, visited me. He had been in the vicinity and wanted to visit me before his return. I had the intention to go to my overseer, Anatolij, the one who

accompanied us out in the morning, and take leave of him. But he wa
nowhere to be found. I discovered that he had gone into the camp bi
would soon be back. So I sat down with Brother Reimer and converse
with him in the expectation that the overseer would come by any momen
Actually only a few minutes had gone by when one of the Captain of th
KGB, named Kowalenko, showed up. He came up to me and asked
"Have you asked anyone for permission?" "No! The overseer has ju
gone into the camp and will soon be back. My visitor has only just arrive
here." Then he screamed at me, "Yes, and are you doing it now withou
asking anybody? You are just sitting here and not working? What kind o
a human being is that?" I wanted to explain to him but he would not let m
say a word and kept on scolding me. Brother Reimer had a briefcase wit
him which he now opened up, and Kowalenko searched around in it an
immediately found Reimer's Bible. "What book is this?" "That is m
Bible." "Why do you bring it here?" "I came from 400 kilometer's dis
tance. When I am traveling so far I always take my Bible with me. Th
brother of Abram Hamm lives in my district and sent me greetings t
bring to him." Then Kowalenko leafed through the Bible and found a littl
piece of paper with a Canadian address. "What is this then?" "It is a not
from Canada." Then he screamed at him, "Why are you entangling him
with foreign connections?" "I'm not entangling him with any foreig
connections. The note and address belong to me." After that he foun
some cassette tapes and tried to read the inscription on them. He lettere
out loud the word 'children' and asked, "What is this, 'Children'?
Brother Reimer explained to him in Russian, "These are cassette tape:
for children." "Aha," screamed he, "Here Hamm sits in the concentra
tion camp because of his work among children, and you bring him cas
sette tapes for children here?" Brother Reimer explained to him, "I only
stopped in when I was passing by and did not have any intention of leaving
the cassette tapes here." And I explained to him more fully, "What would
I ever do in this camp with cassette tapes. I do not even have a cassette
player on which to hear them." But Kowalenko was not even listening. He
roared like a wounded lion. Then he took the Bible and the cassette tapes
with him and went with the words, "Follow me!"

　　This is going to be my last day outside of the camp, I thought, And what
will happen now to Brother Reimer? We had to be taken into two separate
rooms where each was interrogated. This investigation substantiated that
everything was really harmless. Unfortunately, a food parcel that Brother
Reimer had wanted to bring me (which was permitted outside the camp

only) was confiscated. He got his own Bible back after many requests, but the cassette tapes remained in custody. After the interrogation I asked Kowalenko for permission to have another few minutes with Brother Reimer. I wanted to find out from him how my brother Jacob and his family were. It was permitted. Brother Reimer was called in and we were allowed in the presence of Kowalenko to converse with each other in Russian. Then we had to part and I was led back into the camp.

I looked once more at all the trees and flowers as I left them behind me, as though it would be farewell. In the evening I thanked my Lord for the beautiful time which he had given me outside of the camp — it was altogether about three months, and for the many visits and for the good food which I had enjoyed in this time. Especially I thanked him for the opportunities to speak with others of our faith and to share with that old lady parts of God's Word.

Chapter 22

Special Commission In The Mountains

I t was the leading of God that despite all this, nothing happened and I was still given a further two months to work outside.

Now a new project came up 70 kilometers from the camp. In the mountains, a recreation center for the pioneers was being built. Of the 22 men in our work brigade, 10 were chosen for this new work. Since we would naturally enjoy even more freedom there, everyone of us would have gladly gone along. I also had this wish when the ten names were read out. However, my name was not among them. This made me very sad because the way to the construction place went by my own village of Ivanowka, and then another 35 kilometers up into the mountains.

However, 10 days later the situation changed. The construction boss who was in charge of this project, was a German and knew me. He was often in my little workshop and we had good conversations about the faith. Now he was interested in the fact that I could build stoves and do glass cutting work. And he asked me if I would like to do this work at the new construction site, for none of his workers had these skills. I was gladly ready for this. "Good," said he, "I will go to the camp chief and ask for you. The next day he said to me, "It's going to work. Tomorrow morning early take your bedclothes and stand ready." I could have leaped into the air from joy. An overseer said to me, "A materials truck is traveling up there! You are to go along!" I thought, So it worked out just as I wished!

There was still bread, grits, sugar, fish, some meat and vegetables to be loaded up for the prisoners, then the truck left. An officer went along in order to transfer me to another officer at the construction site. On the way I asked the officer — he was an Usbek Moslem — , if I could visit my family in Iwanowka, because we were going there to get some sand from the sand pit. He allowed me permission to do that for as long as it would take to load up the sand. My wife gave the driver and the officer six rubles so that they could eat in the canteen at the sand pit. She had actually set aside the forenoon to do some painting in the house, and planned to eat just a little bit with the children.

After two hours these men came back. The officer looked with pleasure at our group of children, and with gleaming eyes he saw how the two youngest, Heinrich and Peter sat on my lap, and climbed over my knees. Then I took farewell from my family again. The foodstuffs they gave me and my bed things were loaded on the truck and I was permitted to come into the cab. Up we went into the mountains. After our arrival there I was delivered by the officer to the overseer at that place. In the evening we were able to breathe the fresh mountain air out in freedom. We were also allowed to do whatever we wanted after work for our rest time. Just so that we would be punctual the next morning at work time.

The next day was Sunday. We had no time off from work since the construction was supposed to be quickly finished. My task was assigned to me — to build two ovens, and to cut glass for the windows. I busied myself first about the windows because we had to stay in the rooms overnight, and it was too cold with no windows. There were no beds there, so we all slept on the floor. Each had a mattress, a pillow, a cover and two sheets.

On this first Sunday we only had to work until 2:00 o'clock. The overseer, with whom I was unacquainted as yet, came over to me because he wanted to get to know me better. He already knew the other prisoners as they had been here for ten days. I said to him at once, "I'm a believing Christian, and for this reason I have been sentenced. My family lives only 35 kilometers from here. May I go to visit them." He answered, "I have nothing against it. Only you be sure to be back here early in the morning, and begin working punctually at 8:00 o'clock. But how will you go down there and back? Here in the mountains a car passes only very seldom." "I shall run to the foot of the mountain. There is a Kirgesian village with a bus station, and the bus travels to our village." "Well and good. Get on the way now!"

Soon I was ready. Hardly had I gone the first part of the 14 kilometer long way on foot when along came a truck. I lifted my hand and he stopped. But he was so fully loaded that it was impossible for me to get on. So I went on and the hope of coming home again gave wings to my feet. After another kilometer a tractor came by with big rubber tires. It had no wagon behind it, and the cabin was completely filled with people.

The tractor driver stopped and said, "I'd like to take you along, but you can see for yourself how it is. It just isn't possible. I can hardly even move myself." I thought to myself, to travel poorly in some kind of vehicle is always better than to walk well! And I said, "I will climb on the back, and that will be fine." "Whatever you think! Jump up on it!" The driver was drunk as I later found out. He traveled with high speed through the many mud holes and chuck holes in the road, and didn't bother himself in the slightest about avoiding them. The dust flew high and I soon looked like a black man. Now and then the driver looked back through the window and asked, "Are you still there?" "Yes, I'm still here." "Good!" But it actually didn't go that well with me. More than once my feet slipped off and I had to hang by my hands until I could get my feet on a secure place once again. Otherwise, I would have been thrown down. In spite of that my heart was full of joy because I was going home. So we came to the Kirgesian village of Beriken and I asked the tractor driver to leave me at the bus stop. I thanked him for taking me along, and he laughed when he saw my dusty figure.

At a water puddle I washed my face and dried it with my handkerchief. Very soon the bus came and I climbed on. After a few minutes it proceeded further. Then a women came walking along who also wanted a ride, so the bus stopped to let her on. I saw through the window of the bus a motorcycle and a PKW in which sat some good friends. Here were Brother Heinrich Wiebe from the village of Kant, Brother Walter Wedel, who is now living in Paderborn, and Brother Oscar Rivinius, now in Villigen. Immediately I got up and got off the bus and greeted the three brethren. Brother Wiebe took me to my home with his motorcycle. The next morning Brother Giesbrecht was ready to bring me back to work again. My wife prepared a meal that I could take back to the prisoners.

As I came once again to the work site the next morning, the prisoners came out of the house to eat breakfast. They hungrily ate up everything which my wife had sent along: bread, cheese, eggs, milk.

Then I busied myself on the work of getting the window glass cut and installed. Hardly was it dark again, when along came a car with three men (one of them was the Secret Service Chief Kowalenko) and they demanded to know immediately, "Who went home last night?" Everything remained still, even I. Then we had to be taken individually for interrogation. I said to the Brigadier, "I only came here just yesterday, so I will wait until last." And he agreed. While the others were taken for interrogation I went out, knelt in the bushes and prayed especially for my overseer who had given me permission to go home. When they all were finished I went in with a heavy heart. Then the officials turned to me. "Ah, you are here now!" said Kowalenko. "Yes," I answered. "I was just sent here on Saturday." "We were just going to interrogate you, but now let that be well enough." They took our overseer with them, and a new one had already been brought along. I could not imagine what was happening. I had thought it was about me! Later I understood from the other prisoners that the overseer on the Friday before I had arrived had permitted a prisoner to go home. This man lived in the vicinity and had misbehaved himself while he was at home by drinking and racing wildly about, so that someone had reported him. The overseer spent five days in the punishment cells and was reduced in rank.

Our new overseer was named Peter. I knew him already, for when he had built his house I had often repaired and sharpened his tools. I asked him if I could go home again on the following Sunday. He said, "That is dangerous, because the prisoners have often betrayed me when I have given one of them permission to do something like that. But there is one possibility. If you would be picked up so that nobody would see it, and be back so early that the others are still sleeping, then I would give permission!" I answered, "I'll arrange it this way." As I received visitors during the week, I made out with the Brethren who should come get me. Everything worked well, and once again I could be back home. On Monday morning at 4:00 o'clock Heinrich Dück, who is now in Espelcamp, came with his motorcycle to pick me up. We traveled to 400 meters short of the construction site. The rest of the way I went by foot. Softly I went into the construction area. All were still sleeping; and I stretched myself on my place directly behind the door and went to sleep.

On Tuesday we were all called together suddenly. We had to roll up our bedthings and tie them. They were thrown into a truck and we all went back to the concentration camp. We had to let everything go even though the construction was not yet finished. Even the windows had to be left unfinished as there was a shortage of glass. Nobody could understand it, but this is the way it often goes in the Soviet Union.

Next I was sent to a kindergarten near the concentration camp. Here I built tools, chairs and toys or repaired them. To be sure, I was not a cabinet maker, but I understood something of this work. A big heap of furniture pieces and toys lay to one side. I brought back into order one piece after another. My wife and my children and even friends visited me there again. I had a reasonably good situation.

Our Brigadier was not inclined to favor me because I had crossed him
once in not supporting him in an evil activity. One day he said to me,
"When your wife and your children are here, you are always praying with
them. That is forbidden!" I took it from what he said that he had reported
me to the chief of the camp. On the 20th of July as we went up to the iron
gate of the camp, there stood the chief of the camp. He examined each
prisoner thoroughly, and checked their brigade numbers on the list. Then
he made a short speech, "We should comport ourselves decently when
we go out. We should keep our camp clothes on and not change into civilian clothes, and with the other people we should only speak of those
things that pertain to our work. Then he let all the others go out of the
camp gate except me. He said to me, "Hamm, you come with me into the
office." There he showed me a seat in a friendly manner and asked me
how things were going with me. Then he put the question to me, "Are you
still praying?" "Yes, of course!" "Do you have Christian literature, and
do you read in it?" "Yes, after work and on Sundays I read in it." "Do you
also have any Christian writing outside of the camp?" "No, I do nothing
but my work outside of the camp, and I do not bring anything along to
read." "Do you speak with other people about your faith?" "Yes, especially gladly if anyone is interested in finding out more."

During this interrogation my work place and my sleeping place were
searched thoroughly. Fortunately I had my Bible in a safe place. I had
given it to another prisoner, one who was not a believer, but who was
friendly with me. While the chief of the camp was still speaking with me
the overseer came in and laid before him a handful of Christian literature
which he had found by my bed. Even poems which I had received in letters were there. Now the Chief turned to me, "Hamm, you have trans-
gressed the orders of the camp. This is a camp of strict punishment. You
have prayed, you have Christian literature, you have held religious conversations with other people, as you yourself have confessed. For that
you will be punished. From now on you may not work outside anymore.
From now on you will work in the sawmill of the camp."

As my relatives wanted to visit me when they expected that I would be
coming outside, they were told, "He is restricted!" But I have to give my
God thanks that he had given me the gift of these five months in which I
could have freer movement and many visits. No one had thought it possible that an unreformed believer could enjoy such good fortune. This was a
blessing of my Lord. And he is still able to do miracles today.

Chapter 23

The Time Before My Release

A s a young boy I had often heard the proverb which says: "It is the length of something that makes it a burden." I could not grasp the concept at that time, but later I learned to understand it. For most prisoners it goes this way in the concentration camp. With each successive year the burden of captivity becomes heavier, and the vexation becomes more and more terrible. Many begin to curse and to groan ceaselessly, and others to give way to despair. Believing prisoners, and I as well, had it somewhat easier. We could experience the presence of our Lord and thus the Savior helped us get through the present with hope for the future. He gave us the power to overcome even the bitterest hours.

One time I tried to shorten the last hundred days of my three year sentence by counting the days. For three long days I said to myself, "Now there are only 99 days, now there are only 98 days, now there are only 97 days." Remarkably it was only these three days that came to seem longer to me than all of the others before. It seemed as though one day just didn't want to go by. Then I said to myself, "Abram, this will never do! In this manner you are going to turn the last three months into three years. You had better start over again. Take some occupation that will surely last for the last three months then the time will go rapidly." So I set myself the task of reading the entire New Testament through from the first to the last page, and in the process to underline all the important passages. Besides that I wanted to speak to some more of the prisoners about faith in the Lord Jesus Christ, especially with three Germans whose welfare I had on my heart. Now my free time after work began to go so quickly that I thought the time would hardly reach to accomplish all this which was projected.

Always when release from prison was imminent, most of the prisoners found that it affected them with much unrest. The nights before their release they could hardly sleep at all. And in the last night not at all.

I experienced once the same thing, and yet something even more strange. Several prisoners were released at the same time. They stood at the gate and waited for one who was not yet there. His name was announced on the loud-speaker, but he had not yet appeared. Finally, the overseers and guards searched all the barracks until they found him. They drove him to the gate and there he was asked, "Well now, man, what's the matter with you? You are now free!" He answered miserably, "What shall I now do with this freedom? I have nobody who cares for me. Here in the camp I don't have to be bothered to be responsible for anything. I get my supper and my bread. Evenings I can lay on my bed and have a roof over my head. What then should I do out there in freedom? I don't have anybody left!"

Before I was released I prayed to the Lord, "Make me completely peaceful about it!" This God gave me. My last night in the camp came, and as usual at ten o'clock in the evening all the lights went out. My barracks companions said to me, "Abram, tonight you are not going to sleep!" "I will sleep. You will notice it!" As usual a lot more was said, and then each one slept one after another. Finally everything was still and I also slept.

As I awoke refreshed from a deep sleep, I thought, It is probably 5:00 o'clock in the morning! (For in the camps the prisoners dare not have any watches). Then I stood up and I thanked the Lord that he had given me the force to survive this term in the concentration camp and I went out. The guards who every half hour made their rounds, to be watching for tracks of any escaped prisoners, noticed me and called to me. It was the officer who had saved my Bible for me after I had been discovered reading in on the roof with Walter Vetter. He recognized me and said, "Hamm, what are you doing here?" I replied, "It's already morning isn't it?" "Come on now! It is only three o'clock in the morning!" "I didn't realize that! That comes from the fact that my sentence will be over today. I guess that's why I can't sleep anymore." He replied, "Well, I can really believe that, but here you are not permitted to run around in the night, otherwise they will lock you up in the punishment cell during your last hours. So you better see to it that you disappear!" So back I went into my barracks and lay down once more on the bed. Naturally I couldn't sleep anymore. From such a joyful anticipation my appetite was gone, and I did not go to breakfast.

Around 9:00 o'clock I presented myself at the gate. I had my letters and my German Bible with me. The Bible I would have gladly left with some prisoner in the camp, but no one could read German. At the gate several men collected who would also be released on the 20th of October, 1973. For the last time we were searched. The guard took my Bible in his hand, turned it this way and that and leafed through it and saw that many lines were underlined. But he could not read it so he asked one question after another. Then along came an officer and said impatiently, "What are you doing now so long? Let him go! He is going out into freedom. What do you want to do here any longer. Don't hold us up." Then he finally released me and I stepped out into freedom. The joy which filled me can only be experienced by one who has been robbed of his freedom. "I'm free! I'm free!"

Some of my children came running up to meet me. They had known that this is the day that I was to be released. Then Brother Petker greeted me, and several of the other Brethren of my congregation. We stepped off to one side and thanked God that he had allowed me to experience this day of freedom. Then we climbed onto our motorcycles with sidecars, and after forty minutes I was able to greet my family at home.

8. A thanksgiving feast of the congregation in Iwanowka, in 1965.

Chapter 24

Throwing Stones—
A Clear Message

Maria: Before the young men are taken into the military, they are invited, with their parents, to the officials in order to be presented and mustered. Our son Jacob got a summons in the Autumn of 1972, while my husband was still in the concentration camp. I went with him into the village of Iwanowka to the office of the army.

First Jacob was called into the office, then it was my turn. The officer was friendly, and invited me to take a seat. And then began the conversation. His first question was, "Little mother how did you accomplish it that your children are so well brought up and so obedient?" I did not trust my ears to hear such praise, and thought that I had not rightly understood him. For the believers are usually always scolded. For this reason I said only, "What is that?" Then he repeated the same question once again.

I answered, "How can you know if our children are really obedient and well brought up?" "That we see immediately in a young man. You can tell what kind of training he has had at home. Your son sits quietly and handles himself respectfully. He answered modestly and reasonably when he was asked something. By this one can see what is in a young person. How many children do you have?" "Nine," said I. Whereupon he looked into the papers and answered, "That figures." "Do you work?" he then asked further. "I have worked in the sugar beet fields. Now I cannot do it anymore because I have to remain at home with the children and we do not have any Kindergarten in our place." "What does your son work at?" "He works days in the forest school and evenings he is taking the tenth class in night school." "Why does he do that in the evening and not during the day?" "Well, there is no other way he can do it. He has to help earn money so that all my children can be supported."

"Well good," he said further, "But now I have to ask you for the second time; how do you bring it about that the children are so well brought up?" "I don't know if they are brought up better than the other children in our area." "Yes, they are that. And what do you do for their education?" I answered, "Most crimes and sins are committed in the dark. Do you believe that?"

He looked at me reflectively and said, "There you are right." Further I said, "For these reasons we do not allow our children to run around outside in the dark. Only if I am going with them somewhere or if I know where they are do I allow them to be out in the evenings." I thought also of attendance at our evening worship services. But of that I didn't want to say anything. Then I continued on to say, "A few days ago I was with my son and oldest daughter and we went out in the evening. I came back somewhat earlier and waited for both of them. Since they did not come right away I was somewhat restless and listened to see if I could hear their footsteps nearing. Then I heard a noise at our wall outside, and it seemed to me that they must be standing there together with neighboring children. Then I noticed that it was not my children. Two youths stood at the entrance and were looking around to see if anyone was coming. Another youth went out into the street. Probably he wanted to steal the little bicycle of our children's. I knocked hard on the window. Then the other two called to the boy out in the street, "Come back!" and threw a stone against the window. Our double window smashed above my head and the stone flew into our kitchen. The bed which stood under the window was full of glass splinters, and in that bed slept two of our children, Elizabeth and Helen. These three evil doers were boys from the 5th and 6th class. I knew who they were but I kept myself from reporting them for they would only have damaged us further the following evening. Besides that, my children have had to suffer from those three in the school. If all parents would not allow their children to run around in the dark, then there would truly be fewer criminals."

The officer interrupted me, "Yes, you probably have the right idea there. But that you did not report these boys is not right!" "Comrade officer, I could not have reported them, or they would have beaten my children into cripples and we would have had no single unbroken window. It was not the first time that they had stoned us. In our roof there are several holes caused by the throwing of stones."

"Alright. Where does your husband work?" "He is not at home. He is in a concentration camp because of his belief in God." "What? Because of his belief in God?" "Yes! We are believers." "But you may be believers; and nobody is put into prison because of belief. He must have done something else." "No," said I, "We are believers of the Baptist Brethren Church." I thought when he heard the word "Baptist," everything would be clear to him.

"Yes," said he, "But in spite of that nobody is ever put into prison because of their faith." Then I answered him, "It was not long ago here that we had a three day trial in Tokmak because of my husband and two other Brethren as well as one Sister. Everyone who had something to say was invited. And you don't know about it? How can that be!" "I really know nothing about it," said he. "But that's remarkable," I ventured. "Where do you live then? Probably not in the Soviet Union if you don't know anything about this!" "Naturally I live in the Soviet Union," he replied. "Behind Iwanowka in the brick factory is where I live." "And there you have learned nothing about this? That is hard to believe!" But he remained with his assertion and said, "There has to be something else against your husband than just belief." "That's the main charge," said I. "And in addition to that it happens that we were accused of having gatherings of our congregations in our house." Now he began to question what was preached there. I said, "You can gladly come and listen to us. We preach the Bible, Christian songs are sung, and prayer is made. Everyone can come to us freely, whether poor or rich, whether young or old." "Aha, even children?" "Yes, of course! We want to be saved and have our children saved, too." "Well, there we have it then; it is because of the children." Then I replied to him, "God requires us parents to train up our children in the way that they should go. But this is not required of you!"

Then he said, "You are surely too strict with them. They dare not have either movie, theater or television. How can the children learn in school?" "That is different. In a way it is better, in a way not as good; but as for discipline, no teacher has yet complained about them." "But that is still a great plus, that is good," he said. "And are the children part of the Pioneers?" "No!" I answered. "But that is not good," he cried. I answered, "A Pioneer dare not believe in God. But we believe in God. For that reason we cannot send our children with the Pioneers."

Then a lady came into the office and said, "Excuse me please if I am disturbing you. I just wanted to come in and get something out of the file." He replied, "That's alright, I was already finished with the matter. I only had a couple of questions yet for Frau Hamm which interested me!" "Aha", I thought, "this finished it!" I stood up and asked, "I suppose that is all you want to know concerning my son?" "Yes", he answered, "I have nothing more to ask about that. But it still interests me what is preached in your churches." "Good, if you are interested, just read the Bible, for it is all written in there! Or ask others who understand Russian better than I do. May I go now? I must go to the Post Office yet before it closes, and to my children for they are alone." So he dismissed me.

One year later on the 9th of December 1973, the wedding of Maria, our oldest daughter, took place with a believing young man from our congregation, by the name of Cornelius Martens. For this we had called the whole congregation, as well as a number of believers from other areas, and invited them to our house. (There was a total of over 300 persons.)

Across our yard and behind the house the supports of a large tent were set up. Under this we had our wedding feast. In the evening before when the preparations were finished we closed the week with a blessed prayer meeting. Nobody interrupted us, not even the authorities, and for this we were happy and thankful. After that, most of them went home. Only the young people stayed behind because they wanted to decorate the space where the celebration would take place.

Just at this moment my husband's three sisters arrived from Orenburg. They also wanted to take part in this great wedding. We welcomed them with great joy. Since we did not want to disturb the youth as they went about their work, we sat in the bedroom and exchanged remembrances about the old days, after we had put the children to bed. All at once there was a loud noise, and we flew outside to see what it was. The double glass window was splintered into pieces, and a stone more than a pound in weight, and larger than an egg had flown straight through both rooms. It hit my sister-in-law's Elizabeth on her elbow, and landed then in the corner. What would have happened if it had hit her on the head.?

I took the children from their sleeping bench and shook out the covers because it was covered with splinters. We searched the bed for splinters so that the children would not cut themselves. At the same time we heard boys running away outside. Our youth followed after them and Cornelius seized one of the evildoers. He knew well how a Christian should handle himself in these circumstances. But this time he could not hold himself back and he gave the culprit a few hefty blows on the ear. This was something he told us only later. He also took a can of gasoline away from him. What the boy had in mind to do with that we never knew. We could only suppose that he would have wanted to set the house on fire, or make a fire beside the house to scare us.

So we had to experience many hard things, especially through the years of 1970—1973, when my husband was being held. The windows on all four sides of our house as well as the roof was beaten in with stones in various places. Why was this? Because we belonged to the Lord, and we thanked him for having given us the provisions so that we could build a house. Then, too, weren't we a thorn in the side to the communist youth and the officials? We were very thankful to our God that he led us through all persecutions, searches, separations, blows, mockery and scorn (even in the school). I will never cease to pray for the persecuted Christians all over the world, as well as for their persecutors.

Chapter 25

Emigration

Abram: Approximately from 1960, new hope came to many Germans in the USSR; hope of resettlement. Single families actually were able to leave the country. The longing for Germany lived in many of them, but not much was spoken about it because memories about what had happened in the 1930's and in World War II were still too fresh. In those days the hatred of the Germans was very great.

To me personally not the slightest thought of emigration abroad had come. But at the beginning of 1973, while in the concentration camp, I received a letter from my wife. She wrote that the people were speaking about how the Germans could now emigrate to resettle, and wondered whether we could also have this hope. I answered her that she shouldn't believe such talk because we had been deceived before. But towards the end of my time of punishment in the camp my wife became very restless. She had heard that during the night whole trains were being put together, and then the call would be coming; "Leave everything here. Let it lay, and just take a few little things with you!" Many Germans said, "And if I have to leave in my underclothes, I am ready to leave!" Because of this my wife was afraid that they might have to go on the train and leave without me. What should she do? Without me she did not want to travel. But to remain behind was also bad, as there may never be another opportunity to get out of there.

I myself did not think there would be a wholesale resettlement of Germans, and so I tried to calm my wife. The whole rumor came from the fact that the clauses of the Helsinki Pact were not wholly understood. Breshnev had promised that families who had been torn apart during the war would be allowed to come together again.

After my release from prison in October, 1973, I was called into the officials several times, and interrogated about my congregational work. I was asked what office I had, and whether I was still working in youth and children's work, and whether I was involved in welfare work for suffering families. Suddenly I was asked if I would like to travel out of the country. I affirmed this, but also admitted that I did not have any near relatives in West Germany. Then they said, "Just give us an address there!" Therewith they gave me to understand that it was all one to them whether it was a near relative or a distant acquaintance. Through a distant relative in West Germany, Johann Hamm in Verl, near Gütersloh, I then arranged to be asked for. I had to fill out various questionnaires, and already after two months, by the end of November 1974, we received the permission to emigrate. Within ten days we were supposed to be ready to leave!

Before the whole congregation I asked if they would be agreed to my resettling abroad. The congregation answered, "If God opens the door for you, then travel calmly out. We all have the wish to return to the land of our forefathers."

Our children, however, were made anxious by the teachers in the school. They claimed, "In West Germany there is no bread and no meat for you. There you will have to suck on bones and nibble and gnaw in vain on them. Shoes and clothing you will not be able to have, because only the higher classes can afford them." But we did not let ourselves be fooled. We already had many letters from West Germany and through them we learned that it was actually much better than here. Naturally we did not expect heaven on earth. The devil was going about like a roaring lion in the Soviet Union, and trying to destroy the believers through bloody persecution, and brutal oppression, but he was not able to destroy as many as he has been through the temptations for prosperity, and the freedoms of the West.

On the 9th of December 1974, it had developed so far that my wife, I and our children (our son Jacob was in the military at this time) climbed on the train in Iwanowka in order to embark on our journey to the homeland of our forefathers. Many believers and also unbelievers accompanied us to the place of our departure. Once again thoughts rose in me. "Will I ever be able to see this village and all these familiar faces again?"

We traveled next to Moscow, and spent overnight there in a hotel. On the next day I joined a long line in front of a store to buy some oranges. Actually I had some luck and was able to buy about two pounds for the children. These were the first oranges they had seen in their lifetime.

Then we could finally leave the Soviet Union. On the 12th of December, 1974, we arrived in West Germany.

With great thankfulness, I may say that here in West Germany we were received as human beings. Overall, they have stretched to welcome us with a helping hand. Even as soon as we reached Friedland, we were received warmly by the Red Cross and by church representatives. Right from the first day on, we received greetings from the government, and unemployment money. Something like this we had never experienced in the USSR. There we had to do the hardest labor, especially in the years of forced labor, and not even once received a decent wage for it. As we left from the USSR we brought with us only a few suitcases for nine persons. For each person we were permitted 90 rubles, about 308 Deutch Marks). This we could take along and exchange into German money.

In Bielefeld we received temporary lodging. But even in that, there were ordinary beds with good bedclothes. The officials, the Red Cross, the church helpers, and private persons all helped us and we could only be astonished at so much readiness to help and so much friendliness. We were filled with thanksgiving to our God and for him because he had fulfilled our longing to return to the homeland of our fathers. Now we were in dignified and humane circumstances, and in freedom at last.